Unless You're a Hermit Success Means Working with People

by
James Akenhead, ED.D.

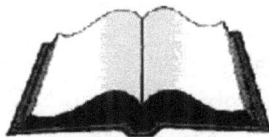

CCB Publishing
British Columbia, Canada

Unless You're a Hermit Success Means Working with People

Copyright ©2008 by James Akenhead
ISBN-13   978-1-926585-07-9
First Edition

Library and Archives Canada Cataloguing in Publication

Akenhead, James, 1943-
Unless you're a hermit success means working with people /
written by James Akenhead – 1st ed.
ISBN 978-1-926585-07-9
1. Interpersonal relations. 2. Success in business. I. Title.
HF5386.A571 2008   650.1'3   C2008-906607-3

Publisher: CCB Publishing
             British Columbia, Canada
             www.ccbpublishing.com

To Our Granddaughters
Lauryl & Samantha Akenhead

Contents

Introduction 1

    Your Personal Model 1

    A Sounding Board 1

1. The Basics 3

    A Concrete Approach 3

    Prevailing Paradign 4

    Origin of Ideas 4

    The Biggest Challenge 4

    Leadership 5

    Formal & Informal Power 6

    A Game Plan 6

    Rules of the Game 6

    Basic Operating Principles 7

    Building Chips 9

    Long-Term Success 9

    The Feel-Good Mentality 10

    Developing Trust 10

    Time for Process 10

    Establishing Boundaries 11

    Interest and Expertise 11

    Understanding Momentum 11

2. Be a Team Player 13

    But, What If… 13

    Structure of Teams 14

        The Best Kind of Team 14

        Team Formats 14

        Other Structures 16

    Maintaining Cohesiveness 17

    Realistic Expectations 18

3. Be a Team Developer 20

    Identifiable Stages 20
    Recycling and Rebuilding 25
    Task and Process 25
    Necessary Leadership 27
    Mission 27
    Point Team 28

4. History as Foundation 30

    Analyze the "Films" 30
    Interview Strategy 30
    The Right Questions 32
    Manage Judgment 35
    Avoid Paranoia 36
    A Plan for Training 37

5. Personal Style 38

    Identifying Style 38
    Components of Style 39
    A Best Style 40
    Talk versus Relationship 40
    Style, Comfort, and Competence 41
    Style and Job Expectations 42
    Style Assessment 44
    Choosing Instruments 47

6. Belief Systems 50

    The Little Voice in My Head 50
    A Computer-Based Analogy 51
    Cultural Awareness 57
    Just Give Me the Facts 58
    Flexibility 59
    Impact on Motivation 59

7. Intangible Elements 61

General Areas to be Considered 61
Scales for Specific Evaluation 63
    Knowledge Rating Scale 63
    Experience Rating Scale 64
    Commitment Rating Scale 65
    Fear Rating Scale 65
    Integrity Rating Scale 66
    Empathy Rating Scale 67
    Originality Rating Scale 67
Tabulation and Scoring 68
Analysis of Results 69
Debriefing 69
Make a Plan 70

8. Intuition and Gut Feelings 71

A Rational Basis 71
Intuition and Reality 72
The Reliability of Intuition 72
A Structure to Work with Intuition 72
Where Intuition Takes Place 75
Enhancing Intuition 76
Results of the Intuitive Effort 78
In "The Zone" 80
Risk Assessment 81
True Leadership 81
Presenting Results of Intuition 82
How People Respond 82

9. Foundation Skills 84

Fundamental Skills 84
    Problem Analysis and Assignment 84
    Developing Support and Helping Skills 85
    Self-Disclosure and Confrontation 86

Behavior, Labels, and Language 87
Productive Dialogue 87
Solving Problems 88
Stages of Skill Mastery 91
Blissful Ignorance 91
Now I'm Really Uncomfortable 92
I Think I've Got It 92
Smooth and Integrated 92
Refinement 93

10. Agreement and Integrity 94

Agreements 94
Maintaining Integrity 95
Grinding Through Old Stuff 96
Really Deep Debris 96
Constructing a Playbook 97
Inclusion and Camaraderie 98
Avoid the Set-Up 99

11. Maximizing Talent 100

Follow the Playbook 100
Continuous Evaluation 101
Beware of the Moving Target 102
Player Accountability 102
Player Development 103
Title versus Functions 105
Establishing Boundaries 105
Trouble Spots 106
Rookies 107
Mentoring 107

12. A Better Game Plan 109

Scout the Opposition 109
Organized Practices 109
Changes in the League 110

Dress Rehearsals 110
Listen to the Players 111
Popularity of the Coach 112
Empowering Your Team 113
In Touch with the Owners 114
What Works 114

13. Constant Improvement 115

Practice Formats 115
Processing and Debriefing 117
Action Activities 118
The Total Communication Picture 119
Props and Tools 121

14. Time as Context 122

Personal Perception 122
Feelings and Philosophy 123
Adding Structure 123
Mutual Needs 124
At Peace with Time 125

15. Acknowledgment and Unity 127

Personal Acknowledgment 127
Group Acknowledgment 128
Send it Home 129
Written versus Verbal 130
Directing Focus 130

16. Marketing and Perception 132

Subtle Communication 133
A Marketing Plan 134
        Public Relations Project List 135
Planning Sequence for Marketing 136
Where to Focus 138
Marketing as Manipulation 138

Spotlight Talent 139
Celebrate Victories 139

17. Focus Groups and Forums 141

Size Makes a Difference 141
Staff Discussion Groups 142
Tips on Process 147
Outreach Forums 148
Organization and Logistics 149

18. Facilitation and Consensus 150

Win, Lose, or Draw 150
A Matter of Opinion 150
Judging Decisions 151
Why It Works 151
No Panacea 152

19. Stress and Self-Preservation 154

What Works for You 154
Finding the Formula 155
Maintaining a Balance 156
Capitalizing on Support 159

Appendix 160
Changepoint Perception Assessment 164

References & Resources 172

About the Author 175

Introduction

No matter what; passion, courage, and persistence are critical elements for success. But alone, these attributes can produce a broad range of results. It is your leadership approach and personal model that determines if you will be successful in relationships; as a sole proprietor; or as the CEO of a larger more complex organization.

Your Personal Model

Your model is a pattern of elements that you use in your daily life, presumably to help you be successful. It doesn't have to be fancy and you may not even be conscious that it exists. It involves everything you do. Including, but not limited to: what you believe, how you act, how you talk, how you dress, how you take care of yourself, and how you solve problems. All these things contribute to your success and satisfaction. By becoming conscious of your personal model you take more control of your life.

A Sounding Board

This book provides you with a framework and offers specific elements as a blueprint for you to examine your own model. In short, it provides a sounding board to help you identify your personal approach; it challenges you to search for the "why" in what you do and it helps you to identify an overall operations model.

Unless You're a Hermit Success Means Working with People

1

The Basics

Going on a trip often means taking an airbus to the desired destination. As we make the flight, our liner may be off course much of the time. It is only the continuous corrections made by the pilot and crew that bring the flight in on time and on target.

It is this same ability to make course corrections that brings about success in relationships and professional endeavors. Without attention to when correction is needed, it is often pressure that brings it about. This stress may come from perceptions about mismanagement, use of money, disharmony, low morale, or a mismatch of goals and values.

When pressure of this kind exists, the first priority is to bleed it off or avoid an impending collision. Unfortunately, once relief is felt, we all too often return to business as usual. When this path is chosen, there may be little chance for real change.

To get solid success over the long term requires us to be aware that organizations, even families, must make constant corrections, sometimes even when things appear to be going smoothly.

A Concrete Approach

For decades attempts have been made to determine what contributes to success. Unfortunately specific elements have been hard to identify. Instead, the most identifiable success factor seems to be the individual who attracts admiration or loyalty through power or personal charisma. Although success via this venue seems undeniable for some, others need a more concrete model that works over the long haul.

Prevailing Paradigm

When we choose to become conscious of our personal approach, the first challenge is to accept the idea that people may need to learn new skills and concepts instead of assuming that they come equipped with all that is required. For some, **it's almost as if there is a paradigm that prevents even the consideration that we need to develop skills and understanding in order to function more effectively.**

Origin of Ideas

Building a personal model involves bringing together thoughts and ideas that have been tried and reworked by many people in varied circumstances over considerable time. In pulling together a model of this kind, it is important to remember that it must be open to evaluation and change. At each occasion when it appears that all needed parts are present, new dimensions emerge, sometimes very simple and sometimes from surprising sources. When this happens, it does not mean that the overall structure should be discarded. Nor, does it mean that the existing structure should be an excuse for not making a meaningful change.

And finally, in spite of the shortcomings that exist in any model, it's wise to consider the possibility that **any well thought out working model is preferable to allowing the future to be governed by chance.** This can mean that even small things done at the right time can make a difference which increases our odds for success.

The Biggest Challenge

In a continuing effort to improve an operating model, the biggest challenge we face may be in the realm of **"what we don't know that we don't know."** This is what causes the predictable discomfort that comes with new or unfamiliar territory. It is this

4

discomfort that stops us from taking action to move a new idea to implementation. Becoming comfortable with discomfort is required if we are to develop effective models to live by.

Leadership

Willingness to face the wind rather than turn back for protection. Being driven to search the fringe of what's normal for anything that might enhance your situation. Thinking about everything from a context of how it could be used to make things better.

Combine these with the discipline to mentally fit new information into an already working model and you have key traits of successful leaders.

Leaders facing the wind are looking out, away from their comfort zone, searching for answers, when the norm is to look to the status quo for support. When the norm is to gather with others to exclaim how bad things are, leaders discipline themselves to obtain diverse points of view from other levels of operation or completely different structures.

Searching the fringe requires intentionally looking for the unusual view, the meaning behind the most irritating criticism or the ideas of creative and critical thinkers who challenge the very foundation of our accepted wisdom. It means exploring the most uncomfortable scenarios in order to consider the good that might be buried therein.

Being open to possibility requires the mental discipline to consider that anything we encounter might ultimately fit into our model and that new answers can come from any source.

Being responsible requires trying the strange or new in personal experience. At first, in situations where results are more predictable, emotions are low, and positive gains will not be jeopardized. And later, moving to more complex applications, which are more emotionally laden, and where the stakes are potentially higher.

Formal & Informal Power

As a member of any organization, (even a family) with a specific set of values and goals, one of the keys to success will be to keep in touch with both formal and informal power sources. The formal structure is where there are clear reporting relationships and decision-making powers. The informal structure, often a matter of who can influence others, is not visible and if you don't understand it you are the one at a loss.

If you observe carefully, the way the two structures operate will show up clearly. In each situation, success will be partially accomplished through the formal structure, including official actions, and partially via the informal structure. Our success requires maintaining credibility in the both structures.

A Game Plan

Bringing a model to life and keeping it alive requires its continuous application to everything. It must be continually evaluated as to what has worked and where vulnerability exists. The life force of a model comes from keeping it in our face all of the time.

Professional athletes know that to be successful they must understand every aspect of the game. These rules govern participation in the contest and off the court. The rules can be formal or informal and they may or may not be written. Rules can be about the technical aspects of the game or about expectations for behavior that reflect on an individual or the organization off the field. Respected players learn and follow the rules of their game.

Rules of the Game

Each environment has its own set of rules, and these rules may or may not seem fair or logical from one's personal point of view. If we follow the rules the potential for success is higher. If we don't, more trouble shows up.

By looking at a situation in terms of "the rules of the game," it's easier to depersonalize reactions to the unpleasant aspects; at least until such time as we can influence the changes we prefer.

Basic Operating Principles

To look more specifically at rules, here is a list of important concepts that apply in almost every situation.

1. **Take no action without good reason.** When the pressure is high, the temptation is to do something, even if it is wrong. The most difficult thing may be to sit tight until a helpful course of action becomes clear.

2. **Hierarchy & bureaucracy create perspectives.** Yet, location in the hierarchy is not necessarily related to intellect or knowing the right answer.

3. **Dignity of the individual must not be defaced.** There is nothing that will undermine a sense of community more than taking away dignity.

4. **Act on the problem, not the person.** It's sometimes difficult to separate emotion from fact. If this is not done, reaction may be more about retaliation than how to resolve problems.

5. **Resist inflicting personal values.** Instead create an awareness of your values and the reasons for them while also working to understand the values of others.

6. **Exhibit patience and empathy toward others.** People need to be heard and acknowledged. The first element in successful problem resolution is gaining clarity.

7. **When an organization represents people, power comes from those served.** The consequences of this principle are predictable.

8. **There is always more than one option.** When we believe otherwise, it may be a sign we haven't yet looked hard enough.

9. **Bosses & Boards of directors make judgments.** Judgments represent choices. Choices represent valued-based decisions. The success of these decisions is related to the quality of information that is available.

10. **The role of a leader is diverse.** It includes identification of problems, visualization of future needs, management of logistics, collection of research, formation of options; identification of consequences, development of recommendations, listing of prioritized options, and implementation of decisions.

11. **People support what they understand and what is important to them.** We need to listen to people to know what they think and feel.

12. **People need education about what's happening and about their options.** The earlier an issue can be identified, the higher the probability it may be resolved with low conflict.

13. **People can understand the concept that we either pay now or pay later.** This does not mean we can dictate what others must "buy" and we can provide a process to help evaluate choices.

14. **To be successful, one must win more than 50% of the time.** To do better than chance requires a conscious approach to all aspects of life.

Building Chips

In his book on self-esteem, Jack Canfield spoke of a concept called the "poker chip theory." To build on this idea, imagine a stack of chips with a value that changes each time a decision is made. If a decision falls within the acceptable range of the value system of those in control, or those served, chips are added to the pile. Each misjudgment costs one or more of those chips. Being on target more than off, builds chips. Enough accumulated chips can provide a buffer for the inevitable unpopular or uncomfortable decision. The chances of survival are higher when there are chips to cash.

Long-Term Success

Achieving success doesn't usually mean creating a break-through. Rather, it's often the little things, accomplished by many, added together like bricks in a wall, which make the difference. The strange thing is that when people operate from this point of view, little accomplishments keep accumulating until people realize that they have had a part in building something special.

What Can We Expect from Ourselves and Others

Almost every person is capable of doing far more than he or she believes. The important thing is to know when we are dealing with emotions and doubts that are unfounded versus when we are legitimately at the edge of our physical or emotional ability to produce.

The issue of peak performance for us may not be much different than for Olympic athletes. With Olympic athletes the skill levels of competitors are sometimes so closely matched that the ability to manage self-doubt, debilitating emotion, and negative self-talk can make the difference between taking home a medal and going home empty-handed.

Most of the time, when we feel overwhelmed we can still

continue if we are in a supportive environment. Recognize this and be willing to discuss your situation with your supporters. This creates the atmosphere necessary to meet high expectations and solve our own problems.

The Feel-Good Mentality

One thing that seems consistently difficult to deal with is "the feel-good mentality." It seems that the biggest resistance to any move forward ties directly to how comfortable we feel about it.

Few things can be as troublesome as the idea that if something doesn't feel good it shouldn't be done. It can mean that if you are considering a tough decision that may cause discomfort, maybe it won't be made, no matter what the costs in the long haul.

Developing Trust

Nothing happens in a vacuum. Everything that has been done in the past contributes to or detracts from the number of chips available to cash in the current or next situation. If a trust level has been built by prior actions, people may give you the benefit of the doubt when a hard decision comes down.

Time for Process

When making important decisions, allowing sufficient time for the development process insures the opportunity for proper homework. It allows for collection of relevant data on all sides of the question. It gives people time to explore various options, and it allows for acceptance when there may be some discomfort involved.

Establishing Boundaries

A clear survival issue in today's world centers on being clear about legal options. In a nutshell, you can't afford bad legal advice and it goes without saying that you aren't safe with no legal advice. With that in mind, the first thing required when considering anything new is to establish the boundaries that confine you. That means identification of the specific legal factors that control your actions. Next, identify the values that must be taken into consideration. Finally, consider the available sources for data or research that can bring integrity to the decision-making process. If any of these things are missed, there is potential trouble ahead.

Interest and Expertise

As the opportunity occurs to pick partners, success rate can be enhanced if people chosen have both an interest in the project and the expertise necessary to make it work (Hoy and Miskel). These two criteria can be applied to specific projects or when selecting individuals to become permanent team members.

Interest is an important criterion because it is from interest that a positive attitude and energy may be generated. Expertise is important because energy and activity that is not appropriately directed can be very inefficient. In fact, misdirected energy can actually cause problems for other team members.

If you can't find those who possess both interest and expertise, there is a dilemma. Do you take on someone who has the expertise but will need to be motivated or do you pick an interested person who must be educated? In either case, you will need a plan to fill the void.

Understanding Momentum

Momentum is a concept that provides insight about the time it can take to turn around a system or a relationship with problems. It explains how, once positive motion has been attained, it can regress if effort is relaxed. This backslide begins when the things that were consciously done to create positive momentum begin to be overlooked, ignored, or intentionally abandoned.

The trap is that once people get relaxed with the idea that things are going "well," it is easy to settle in and let things drift. It appears that this happens as people get comfortable with the status quo, thus making the effort that it took to achieve success no longer seem necessary. This subtle desire to stay in a comfort zone puts chance in the driver's seat and ultimately allows the positive momentum to slow, stop, and eventually be reversed.

How fast momentum can be changed depends on the critical nature of the circumstances. If people see problems and believe that their survival is at stake, movement is faster. If people are in denial or don't think the problems will cause them trouble, it can take longer to put forth the effort to counter negative momentum.

2

Be a Team Player

If you are one who recognizes that no one does it alone, working consciously to develop a team mindset can become a great asset. If you see value in this,   "Where do I start?" is often the first question. When it's about dealing with an organization, the answer is "start at the top". In the best-case scenario, that means start at the top of the hierarchy. If that won't work it means start at the top of whatever structure you can influence.

But, What If...

Don't buy the story that if those at the top aren't interested it can't be done. It can be done as long as those working together know their environment, including its politics, and make decisions that include all relevant factors from both the formal and informal system.

There is proof of this everywhere. All we need to do is look close at that exceptional group where things get done; people talk to each other about problems, enjoy going to work, celebrate success together, and give others credit when things are accomplished.

These exceptional teams work because the people on them are able to figure out what it takes to be seen as successful. They learn who needs to be stroked as well as whose toes should not be stepped on. Good teams include all of those things as pieces of data in their planning processes.

No matter what the focus of a team, its members must always know what will be used as the judgment criteria for success. Equally important is the recognition of factors that will get them in trouble. In that way all teams deal with a similar reality.

Structure of Teams

To define a team is to recognize that it is not a thing. Rather, it is a group of individuals in the constant process of getting better or worse at working toward goals.

This definition is a reminder that in a rapidly changing, often chaotic, environment there is no status quo. A team is either gaining maturity and creativity as it resolves problems, or it loses ground and can be overwhelmed by the problems of the day.

The Best Kind of Team

As in the world of sports, there are different organizational designs to accomplish different goals. The nature of the football team is much different than that of a track team, wrestling team, or basketball team. Each desires to accomplish a particular mission. Differences among them exist because missions are different. The psychological factors, structure, skill foundation, and knowledge base must all be organized and focused to accomplish the specific mission and goals of the team.

Team Formats

To help think about the best way to organize a team, here are several analogies. As these scenarios are considered, remember they are only examples. There is no best team configuration except the one that fits your needs.

The Large Group or "Football Team" Format
One way to look at a team structure is to compare it with a football team. Those who watch football know that large numbers of people must be well coordinated in order to make things work.

There may be three or more groups of players that must be linked together in units. Some of these players are assigned to more than one of these groups. Each of these groups must be highly motivated, skilled, and rehearsed until the grace and synchronicity of a ballet company are accomplished.

If one member of that team doesn't know the plays or cannot carry out a personal responsibility it not only jeopardizes the performance of that player, it also jeopardizes the ability of the team. It can be as simple as: if the guard doesn't know when or how to pull and block for the running back, then the timing and success of every other player on the team is impacted. In such cases, the work of some teammates becomes harder while that of others becomes meaningless.

If your environment is chaotic or unorganized, a football analogy may be a good model to use early on. Operating in this format initially requires a substantial commitment of resources. This is because you work with a larger block of people who will be trained in the basic skills and concepts that will become part of your team's model. These conditions require a high-energy commitment on the part of the "coach" or captain as well as a commitment to the time necessary to make the team a smooth functioning unit. If you are working with a team that has a large number of direct service personnel, this may be the perfect format to use.

The Smaller, "Golf" or "Track Team" Format

As in all other facets of operation, the issue of cost for team development and maintenance needs to be considered. Circumstances must be continually monitored to determine when different approaches are more efficient. Alternate structures can be compared to organizational systems like golf or track teams. In these kinds of teams, there is a unified mission; however, the structural workings are different than those of a football team.

These differences are related to how the skills and knowledge of individual members are brought to bear in the contest. On track teams, events are held separately, and then scores are summed to determine the team's total points. A distance runner or relay team may not finish first in an event and yet the high jumper will not be inhibited from completing his or her task.

On a golf team, each member must learn the same skills and compete under the same rules. The difference is that each competes individually. Each match produces a winner, and at the end of the contest the points are totaled to decide which team takes home the prize.

These examples provide organizational formats for consideration. Each can be worthy, depending upon local circumstances. The track team format suggests that a larger team may be broken into subgroups to work in specialty areas. Likewise, a leadership team may subdivide based on an organization's structure, service areas, subdivisions, departments, or levels of administration. With this approach, all personnel are focused on the same goal, coached by the same head coach, exposed to the same team building process, and yet they are subdivided to be more efficient.

The golf team format allows for even more individualization. Each team member must learn the same skills. Each team member is a part of a single focused "whole" and is committed to a particular kind of team culture and relationship. Yet, with all of these things in common, every member makes his or her contribution as an individual.

The golf team analogy may be seen when a team member meets with a client. If the overall team is to be successful, this individual must apply the skills and knowledge learned as a team member and must follow a "playbook" or set of agreements to deal with the situation at hand. If this is done, the credibility of the individual and the team as a whole is maintained.

Other Structures

There are countless models to illustrate different kinds of team options. If you enjoy music, think in terms of an orchestra, its subgroups of instruments, the role of the "first chair," and the soloist. The important point is to recognize that there is not just one kind of team approach. A team can be designed to meet the needs of any situation.

A good start-up is to begin with a larger group. This gets players in alignment on basic skills and processes used for individual and team interaction. Then you can move to formats that require less in total personnel hours, yet provide more specialized training as need in particular units or departments. This initial use of a larger team unit allows members to become quickly involved in decision-making. It allows for the clearing of old problems, better understanding among members, facilitation of a sense of personal ownership, and building of trust.

A change in format works once members of the larger team have confidence that a sub-team can work within the philosophy and utilize the foundation skills, knowledge base, and boundaries that the large team would use

Maintaining Cohesiveness

As teams develop, members should agree on when it is appropriate to make decisions as a team and when it is appropriate to operate in sub-teams or as individuals. As a general rule, the team should function as a whole when breaking new ground. They work in sub-teams or as individual representatives when carrying out activities within the framework established by the team as a whole.

If a sub-team or individual team member encounters a situation that is unique or unanticipated, it might not be resolvable within the parameters established by the team as a whole. In such cases, the individual or sub-team seeks to resolve or ameliorate the situation as immediate circumstances require and then takes that unique situation to the team as a whole for consideration. With this kind of standard operating procedure, team members should be able to rely upon the support of colleagues even if they must occasionally operate outside established parameters. Occasionally is the key word here. If a team member is consistently operating outside of team parameters, it is indicative of a larger problem.

It is easy to underestimate the importance of this concept. Some might say, "it's obvious". And it should be, especially in regard to highly regulated areas. Where it may not be so obvious is in areas where differences might be less likely to be immediately noticed.

For example, if a supervisor lets all staff off early on Fridays or days before a holiday, while others adhere to a standard workday, some get to look like "good guys" at the expense of others. In addition, the staff in some divisions will perceive that they are not being treated fairly. Eventually, this can become a big deal and all because of the way a team communicates and keeps agreements.

Realistic Expectations

Expectations held for a team can set the stage for how things will go. Many believe that if they have a clear vision or goal and are committed to its accomplishment, the path to conclusion will be direct. This is an all-too-common fantasy.

A healthier way to view the path from start to goal is to picture it as a stock market trend chart. People who analyze stocks know that they will have gains and losses. This is an expected part of the process. Successful stock investment rests in identifying trends. If, after examining all of the ups and downs, the trend is up or toward the goal, it is considered a good stock.

As mission, goals and objectives are identified, there will be gains and setbacks. The key to success is if the trend line is moving toward the goal. With this context for evaluating progress, more realistic expectations exist. People can get down on themselves because unrealistic expectations have been set. Because they are committed to work hard, they expect that the path to what is "right" should be straight and involve little resistance. In reality, many good things take time and require navigation around obstacles. These obstacles may have been placed in the path by the

18

system's history, available resources, or as a result of peoples' beliefs.

3

Be A Team Developer

Bringing individuals together does not guarantee that they can coordinate their efforts and influence to overcome the barriers at hand. A group of individuals, even with a clear mission, may go in different directions while attempting to accomplish a desired end. They may even end up at cross-purposes or unintentionally block each other's efforts to reach a goal. This can be true even when every person involved is interested, committed, and energized to get the job done.

Identifiable Stages

To build a team that can effectively work together requires moving through some predictable stages. These stages exist whether consciously recognized or not. Bringing them to awareness helps us understand the dynamics that occur during the process.

Stage 1: The Social Gathering
During this first phase of development, the members of the team operate much like they might at a social gathering. Much attention is paid to titles and status held by others. Almost everyone operates with a close eye to the formal hierarchy. There's much concern about making sure that those with elite university degrees are acknowledged, bosses are treated with a special respect, and those with power in the formal structure may be approached cautiously. People are generally watchful and "know their place."

There are few in-depth discussions during the social phase of team development. When they occur, they are generally among individuals who have already developed a close relationship rather than with the group as a whole. Side conversations may take place between some while others are paying attention to a broader topic being discussed.

This stage of team development is not particularly uncomfortable. In fact, it can be quite enjoyable. This is because almost everything is taking place on what might be considered a superficial level. People's real thoughts and feelings are seldom expressed unless they find themselves in a small intimate sub-group. Trust has not been established to any real degree. Power and special knowledge give people special status. People seldom put themselves on the line for an issue, and very seldom volunteer personal thoughts. This is especially true if they are not sure they have the power base to survive after stating a divergent position.

Perceptions of Power - In this first stage of development, most interactions are based on the participants' assessment of what they have permission to do or say. The importance of having permission is often related to what participants have observed as consequences to others who acted without this permission or what they have directly experienced in the past.

In this stage of development, those with power may assume that if they give verbal permission for others to be open with their thoughts and feelings, an honest outpouring will follow.

Of interest here is that a person with power may assume that he or she is not threatening to others. Then he or she becomes frustrated when people don't immediately open up. The key in such cases is not whether verbal permission has been given. Instead, it is how others perceive the ability and likelihood that reward or punishment will be used. In the first stage of team development, members will carefully test the water to see if what is being said will prove true in real life.

Also assessed by team members, is the history of the system. If history points to sanctions for anyone who has raised questions in the past, team cohesiveness may develop more slowly. Finally, since most interactions during the first stage of development take place on a superficial level, it is the least functional stage. Sadly, for some groups it is the only phase of development that ever occurs.

Stage 2: Confusion

If a group decides to get down to business and make its efforts mean something, a new phenomenon occurs. People begin to consider that this team may be able to actually do more than just put in time. They begin to wonder about what their role might be on a truly effective team. Consciously or unconsciously, they take notice of the styles, values, and beliefs of their teammates. They learn to trust some others on the team and begin to take calculated risks.

During this second stage, confusion often exists, conflict is possible, and discomfort is common. These things are normal because new skills are being mastered, trial and error occurs, and new information is impacting on an organized team effort. In some cases substantial conflict can exist during this second stage. Conflict exists when ideas are stated and not valued, when power is used inappropriately, and when communications are disorganized or censured.

In this stage of development, team members are working to get a clear understanding of how they will fit in and contribute. This is the time when discomfort and confusion cause many teams to turn back and settle for the social gathering as their major operating mode. Getting through Stage Two is the key to having a chance for solid cooperation.

The issues that surface in Stage Two can be as personal as whether powerful people can be called by their first names or asked for reasons behind an opinion. Stage Two also includes gaining an understanding of the type of decision-making practices that will be used and how each member will influence the process.

The best way to approach this stage of group maturity is with the knowledge that it is normal for confusion and some conflict to exist. This advanced notice helps team members to understand that their feelings of discomfort and confusion are also normal.

It is helpful to enter this stage with the expectation that it is a process of sorting issues, roles, beliefs, and personal identities. As part of the team building process, special skills can be taught to help members' progress more quickly and with a lower level of frustration. Creating an acceptance for confusion, even conflict as a normal part of the process is extremely valuable as a team comes to grips with issues that can threaten success.

Stage 3: Putting It Together

If your team survives Stage Two and does not retreat for safety and comfort, a major benchmark has been achieved. Stage Three usually includes a mutual understanding of what the team is doing and how it will be done. More than that, there is a feeling of security in the knowledge that team members are not in it alone. Members have found a niche. Each person has been validated as to his or her style and is allowed to work from individual strength. Each member knows how and when to modify his preferred style to be more effective on the team. Members have had the experience of sharing ideas that have been given full consideration by others on the team. They have shared and explored different points of view, in a structured process, while searching for win-win solutions.

In this stage, there is a sense of energy and excitement about working together. There is a friendliness and sense of pride about being part of something special and perhaps uncommon. In this stage the team often believes that it can accomplish anything.

Because the team gets things done and its members feel a part of each accomplishment, they are willing to spend time and to put themselves on the line. They know that when things get tough, their teammates will be there with them.

Stage 4: Making It Routine

In this stage of development, full maturity is reached. Team members have developed a sense of what should be done in the larger team and what should be done in small groups or individually. There is comfort in knowing that support is available from the team when needed. There are guidelines and agreed-upon structures so that the individual team member knows how to operate when working outside the team while pursuing team goals.

Here, while having security in the knowledge that the team exists for support, members understand that much day-to-day routine must be carried out on one's own or in a sub-group of the team.

In the fourth stage, individuals understand that problem solving and planning are done as a team when dealing with new and unique issues. Once plans have been made and guidelines established, team members can operate independently. If unexpected problems occur, individual members know that they can take them back to the team for consideration. They also know that if they must make a decision in an arena that has not yet been considered by the team, there will be an acceptance level based on trust and understanding.

This trust and understanding is built on the basis that each member honors the mission and operating model of the team in any decisions that must be made independently. This trust is also present because the team understands that no member would intentionally make a decision that would jeopardize the team or go against its operating principles. Members know that the team will be consulted on significant new or unique situations when advance notice is available. At this stage of development there are formal team meetings as well as sub-team structures and loosely structured networking activities, all designed toward achieving the team's mission.

Stage 5: The Delusion

Stage Five exists for people who are still in the social gathering stage and who have convinced themselves that they have worked through the stages of development and are functioning as a closely-knit, highly-effective team.

Teams that have decided to operate from this fantasy perspective are sacrificing the potential expertise and power still hidden in their membership. In teams like this, it is taboo for anyone to get upset. A supervisor or manager may not be allowed to share true feelings with team members for fear of negative fall-out. And, subordinates in the official hierarchy are not allowed to question a supervisor's logic.

Perhaps the saddest part of this scenario is that many of the "leaders" of these teams believe that they have an open, functional operation. Teams that choose to stay in this state are often very verbal about how well they get along and how they have no problems or conflicts among their members. A certain clue that things might not be perfect is when lack of conflict is a substantial criterion for evaluation of success.

Recycling & Rebuilding

Another reality in team development is that members will recycle through the stages of development as circumstances change. This can occur because different demands or problems require reevaluation of basic operating assumptions.

Team dynamics also change when a team member leaves; when a new member comes aboard; or as new skills are learned. In these situations, members re-sort priorities; reexamine personal competency; and reconsider their personal commitment as well as that of fellow members. They then reevaluate their "stake" in the group and its mission.

For these reasons, it is important to provide opportunities for the team to reevaluate its status. The group should periodically identify where it is in the team development process and work through any issues that may impede the ability to do the job that the team exists to perform.

Task and Process

For a team to be successful, there are two essential elements. Over time, a balance of these elements is a necessity if a team is to accomplish its goals.

Task - When dealing with the task element, the group is paying attention to getting the job done through completion of tasks. When dealing with task completion, focus is on setting goals, establishing objectives, doing research, collecting data, and most of all, taking action.

Process - The process element of team operation requires focus on how things are getting done. It requires keeping an eye on the people part of the operation. This means being aware of the kinds of feelings and emotions people are having and how they are affecting the group's operation. In difficult situations, emotions vary as team members come to grips with their personal values and beliefs. Individual views of team members may be pushed and stretched as the group struggles to evaluate information and make a decision that can be supported by all.

Maintaining Balance - The process and task elements are of equal importance. Some teams miss the process element completely. When this happens, team members may build up feelings of anger, insecurity, frustration, or confusion that flood their emotional system. This makes it difficult to stay focused on task related information. Other teams are so process or feeling focused that they compromise their ability to effectively complete the tasks at hand.

In effective teams an effort is made to track process while working on the task. This means knowing how people are feeling about what is going on. It requires that each member be on the alert to what is happening with other team members. It requires that the team be willing to discuss their feelings about team progress and how the team members are going about their job.

If your team is unwilling to deal with either of these elements, the potential for success is diminished. If a team tends to favor one of these elements at the expense of the other, it may be due to the personal style preferences of powerful members of the team.

Necessary Leadership

In today's organizations, leadership must be available at every level and from every participant on the team. Although position titles may infer a position of leadership, in today's fast moving organizations leadership cannot rest in a few individuals. It's time to move past the idea that only a few people, by virtue of their title, automatically know the right thing to do while the rest wait for direction. This change in expectation can cause concern for those who are afraid of power loss and relief for others who may have felt they were expected to perform miracles because of their title.

New emphasis should be on initiation of team action, management of logistics, and facilitation of team decision making. To think of these people as coaches or team captains seems a valid context. A good coach or team captain works to get the best performance to overcome barriers, reach goals, or deal with the opposition.

On effective teams, everyone contributes leadership. This occurs as one's individual energy and skills can be applied to specific situations. Likewise, every member of the team must also be willing to operate in a supportive participatory role. It is this willingness to function both as a leader and supporter that creates the dynamic relationship of a sound working team.

Mission

A professional team must have a mission. In sports, the mission usually includes the desire to win a championship. And it certainly includes a desire to finish at the highest possible level based on league conditions, talent, and resources available. Even with lofty aspirations, the best teams know that they cannot win every time, especially if they are playing in a balanced league where everyone has comparable resources.

Good teams know that to place at or near the "top" on a consistent basis is dependent upon refinements that give them an edge over their competitors. The best also know that even though they may not be able to win every time they can perform in the top five, ten, or twenty percent consistently. This kind of consistent high-level performance assures them of being a contender for success when in competition, or when compared with similar teams. If a work team is to compete at this level, members have got to be clear about what they want to accomplish and how they are going to get it done.

Point Team

A primary goal for those who believe in a team mind-set is to permeate the organization with teams that focus on high quality service delivery in their specialty areas. Each team must be able to function on its own and should have representation on teams that view and interpret the larger picture.

To accomplish this, a decision must be made about who will operate at the "point" of the team development effort. In small or medium size systems it may be possible to involve all line supervisors and managers in the initial team training process. In larger systems, the point group may need to be confined to central administration only because of sheer numbers. In such cases, it is important that those who may be cloistered in a central administration have a sense of reality about conditions on the front lines.

The advantage in small and medium size systems is that the first "cut" at team development can involve representatives from the whole spectrum of operation. It can include central administrators, who are in touch with the big picture; as well as others who know what it's like to fight the battle in the trenches every day.

The value of starting with top management is that once trained and operating as a team, members can serve as visible models for the desired outcomes of team operation. This conveys to others in the organization that top administrators are willing to "walk their talk."

This seems especially important since the perception in some organizations is that top management is forever coming up with ideas about how to fix others without ever taking a look at how they personally operate. If top administrators dive in first and come up modeling what they preach, it is much easier to recruit others.

4

History as Foundation

Analyze the "Films"

Whether you are a veteran coach, a team captain, or a new team member, it's important to analyze how things have been done in the past. In athletics, analyzing films or tapes of past contests and practices as well as looking at data and talking with informed sources does this. In organizations, it is also important that coaches not go forward without having a clear understanding of what has happened in the past. That includes what things have been successful and what things might have been more successful if done differently.

There are at least two ways a leader can do an initial assessment. One way is to use a printed instrument that can be completed by the target audience and submitted anonymously (See appendix Changepoint Perception Assessment). The results from such an instrument can then be used as a guide when designing a training curriculum or to adjust a plan in progress. A second approach involves the use of an interview strategy designed to draw information from key personnel.

Interview Strategy

Using interviews to begin analysis of needs involves talking with those selected for participation on the team; those who might be future participants; and those who have a special perspective. Sufficient time must be allotted for personal exploration with each individual. If the appropriate environment is established, such exploration time can range from thirty minutes to several hours.

No matter how important or scarce time seems, it is vital that someone with credibility spends the time necessary to understand how past efforts have been perceived. This initial interview time can create the opening for people to make a new or renewed commitment. The same type of interview can be valuable in assessing the progress of an ongoing plan.

Setting up Interviews

To create an atmosphere that brings forward the most open and honest dialogue requires a setting where participants do not feel that they will have to contend with conflict or rejection of their ideas. For this reason, individual interviews are preferred. If that is not possible, interviews can be conducted with groups. If establishing small groups, don't forget to look at the informal structure to see who congregate together, eat lunch together, socialize together, and who tend to generally get along in day-to-day operation. Even though this small group approach seems valid, and can be a time saver, it's important to remember that even those who appear to be close friends or colleagues may have differences of opinion which would be better served if explored in private.

Stage Setting for Interviews

Setting the stage for the interview is important. The environment should be as comfortable as possible and the process should be done with an air of informality. This planning helps insure that those being interviewed get a sense that their opinions and ideas are valued. Otherwise, the perception may be that they are being herded through a process, which, by its very nature, suggests they are unimportant.

The Environment - To help accomplish these ends, provide a physical environment where the room and the furniture do not suggest a rigid formal structure. Certainly, this statement will be subject to different interpretations in different organizations because what's considered formal in one may be informal in another. The trick is to make it as informal as possible in a context which people understand.

You may even want to be creative and figure out what one additional step could be taken to make the process even more informal than people are familiar with. For some this might mean moving out of their regular office. For others it might be taking someone to breakfast or lunch to have the conversation.

The Right Questions

Another factor in this kind of information gathering is the use open-ended questions. Open-ended questions allow interviewees to take the discussion where they want it to go. Open-ended questions do not call for yes or no answers. These are the same kinds of questions often used by counselors or psychologists when helping clients explore personal direction.

Question #1: What Has Been Appreciated?

Although you can design your own open-ended questions, this example can provide much valuable information. The purpose is to look for positives to build on. It should sound something like this:

"From where you are now, as you look back at the past, what is it about the way things have been done that you have particularly liked?"

This question allows participants to explore things in the organization that have been supportive of their point of view. The content of the answers from this type of question should give clues about what practices in the organization have been particularly valued and therefore should be maintained in the future, if possible.

Many times when change is considered, there is little emphasis given to the fact that many good things have gone on in the past and that those things can get lost if not protected. Sometimes, it is the maintenance of valued past practices that provide enough stability to deal with changes that may be uncomfortable.

When setting the stage to ask this type of question, it is helpful to start by telling the interviewee that you know there are many good things that go on in the organization. Next, suggest that as we deal with changes that may be required in the future, we want to be sure that we also maintain the things that have been important to success in the past.

This approach validates the idea that people have worked hard and accomplished many positive things. If this step is missed, people may get the impression that managers and administrators are saying that they have not done anything right. This can be a real downer for sincere people who have made a solid contribution to the system and who, if approached in the right way, will be more than willing to work for continued improvement.

As you prepare interviewees to answer the first question, think of how you would like to be approached about your past efforts. Think as well about what it would take to get you to talk about the positive things that have existed in organizations where you have worked in the past.

Question #2: Where Was the Ball Dropped?

A second open-ended question should allow the individual or group being interviewed to suggest changes that they believe would help the organization. A sample question of this type is:

"Looking back from where you are now, and with the experiences that you have had in the organization, what things, if they could be done over again, would you like to have seen done differently?"

This type of question allows people to bring up things that have bothered them about the way the organization has operated and to identify non-desirable outcomes and injustices that they have perceived or experienced. It gives license to deal with negative in a proactive context.

Using this question in a sequence, following the one identifying positive things that should be maintained, establishes a realistic frame of reference. You are conveying that you know there are things that have been positive as well as things that must be changed if the organization is to flourish.

Again, the stage must be set for this question. Ask yourself what an interviewer would need to say in order for you to feel free to identify those things that you believe should be considered for change in the future.

Once these two basic questions have been addressed, the number of additional questions will probably depend upon the amount of time allocated to the interview process. The first two questions can take considerable time if the interviewer creates an environment that encourages people to freely talk about their experiences, feelings, and thoughts.

What Else Do I Need to Know?

Some additional questions for consideration might include:

- *"What do you think will be our biggest challenge in the next three to six months?"*

- *"What do you think will be our biggest challenge as we face the future?"*

- *"What do you think my/our first priorities should be?"*

- *"What do you think my/our biggest problem will be?"*

- *"What could I do that would be of the most help to you in your job?"*

- *"If you were me what would you do first?"*

- *"What do you think others are most concerned about?*

- *"What do you think would make others the happiest or most satisfied?"*

- *"What do you think we could do to increase the quality of our service?"*

- *"As we begin to form or re-form our team, what should be our major focus?"*

As can be seen from this list, a lot of flexibility is available when designing open-ended questions. Again, the key to a successful open-ended question is wording that allows people to focus on their experiences, thoughts, and feelings. A second issue is structuring questions that generate the least amount of resistance from the person answering. Generally speaking when a broad range of possibilities is available when answering the question, less resistance will be present.

In a typical interview, it may be possible to cover three to five questions in a reasonable time frame. A good format includes use of the first two questions followed by one to three additional questions like the examples here. Practice runs can help determine how a question sequence may fit into desired time frames.

Manage Judgment

A helpful approach when conducting this type of interview centers on an understanding of what may be called "passive listening skills." Those skills include the ability to focus on or attend to the other person. This means making eye contact, verbally encouraging the interviewee to continue, and displaying a relaxed body posture that conveys openness to ideas and feelings. It means resisting the temptation to talk about one's own views or to react and explain when ideas expressed create discomfort or strongly align with those of the interviewer. This urge to comment or explain is a big one. Sometimes, it's all you can do to bite your tongue and let the process go on. If done successfully, this conveys that no judgment is being made about a person as he or she speaks in a forthright manner.

Avoid Paranoia

Taking notes about the concepts and ideas identified during interviews will help in later organization. Often, just writing down what people say is a validation of the importance of their ideas and feelings. Sometimes fear and paranoia are so prevalent that anything that could appear as documentation or data to "get them" later can close down the conversation. Before taking notes, ask the interviewee's permission or at least tell him up front that you will be taking a few notes to be sure that you don't lose any important ideas.

A complicating factor is that if you have been with the organization for some time, you may be blind to what is making others in the system feel paranoid. If the potential for paranoia is very high, it may be necessary to use an outsider to conduct this kind of assessment. An outsider can be someone in the system but from a different department who is seen as honest and safe by those who will be interviewed. In other cases this person may need to come from outside of the organization.

If you are new to the organization and are doing assessment as part of your start-up program, you may not have history or "baggage" that will get in the way of your interview process. Recognize however, that your reputation may precede you, and if so, there will be some sort of expectation about how you will operate.

The up side of the process is that many people want to believe that things can get better even if they have not been good in the past. Because of the optimistic attitude that seems to surface as a result of interviews of this type, the information that is obtained can be very valuable in planning an approach to team development.

Long-term success is directly related to whether people perceive the process is designed to manipulate them rather than truly involve them. The approach taken in setting up interviews, creating a good environment, and handling the information received, will all contribute to the perception of your true intentions.

A Plan for Training

Once a target group has been identified, a perception assessment, or interviews have been conducted, and available records have been reviewed, you are ready to plan training. You may want to operate a training camp that attempts to install all basic team formation components at one time or you may wish to operate your camp in shorter segments.

To add to the background information already gathered, the first components of education or training should include the examination of individual operating style and understanding the nature of value and belief systems. These elements apply to the very nature of the interaction among people in all settings.

5

Personal Style

Leaders are quick to say, "people are our most important asset" The question is, how do you take a well-intentioned concept like this and make it concrete enough that you can actually use it to make things work better?

The goal is to make this aspect into an identifiable element in an overall model. To do this involves knowing how we come across to others as well as how our approach impacts both our work and our personal satisfaction. This means we need to know as much about ourselves as possible. We need to understand what kind of behavior we use most frequently and what kind of impact our behavior has in various situations. We also need to know enough about how styles work to be able to identify the basic style of others. Understanding both self and others allows us to make conscious choices as we interact.

A second facet of our persona has to do with our thinking system. It can't be seen and isn't known until it is shared or identified as we make decisions. It is the part of us that has to do with the value and belief systems that act as filters through which we view the world. These filters set the standard of appropriateness for everything we see, hear, or feel.

It is the combination of our style and belief system that determines how we will operate with others, both as individuals and as members of the group. It is this combination of factors and how we manage them that determine our effectiveness in both personal and professional relationships.

Identifying Style

As we consider the foundation of a personal model, there are a number of ways to think about operating style. Some call it a personal profile; others think of it as personality style, personal style, behavior tendencies, or leadership style. While these different names are used as descriptors, what is of most importance is that we know something about how we come across and why we react the way we do, often unconsciously.

Knowing how we come across and how our standard operating procedure impacts others largely determines the way we play out leadership or support roles. In an ideal approach to team participation, when one emerges as a leader depends upon how an individual's interest and knowledge can be brought to bear on the problem at hand.

Given this, each member of the team knows that they will not be in a leadership role at all times. This requires team members to understand how their style shows up in a support role as well as in a leadership capacity. It is the combination of leadership style and support style that makes up our participation style. It is our overall participation style, whether as leader or in support mode, that speaks to our success.

Components of Style

There are two pieces to the puzzle of understanding the impact of operating style. The first piece is personal awareness. Are we high-key and demanding, light-hearted and social, a laid-back "Steady Eddy," or a carefully controlled "Analytical Alice"? We may all possess a little of each of these elements, and it's common to prefer one or perhaps two of these style dimensions over the others. This is not normally a conscious preference. Rather, it's something that we do naturally and without thinking.

Once we understand what our unconscious, natural, and most comfortable operating approach is all about, it's important to step back and look at how our approach fits or conflicts with others. If, for example, we prefer to operate in a very careful and analytical manner, we may be well received by others who prefer the same approach. At the same time we may be creating discomfort for those who move quickly from one task to another in a loosely structured manner.

A Best Style

It's important to recognize that a best style is not being suggested. Instead, we need to recognize the strengths in each person's style as well as where a given style might have vulnerability in particular kinds of circumstances. This understanding enables us to consciously manage our style to enhance success potential.

It is management of style that makes us stronger. It allows us to make conscious choices that will utilize the natural strengths of team members. Knowledge about style differences helps us to realize that when someone approaches a problem from a different angle it is not being done to cause irritation or create a hassle. When we understand that another's style necessitates having carefully analyzed information before making decisions, that need may be easier to accept even if it's different from one's own.

Task versus Relationship

In stressful situations there must be a balance between striving for task accomplishment and building relationships. If a powerful or influential individual pushes hard for task accomplishment without consideration for the human element, he may find that he is without willing followers. Such a leader may be able to coerce others to do tasks while under close scrutiny but they are likely to disengage both mentally and physically when not being closely watched. A more desirable outcome exists when team members commit themselves to the accomplishment of the task because they understand the need and because the human factors have been accounted for as part of the process.

This task-relationship issue can be tied to style because some operating styles seem to focus more naturally on task completion while others focus more on relationship issues. By knowing where a style fits most comfortably with regard to task and relationship, we become aware of the situations that will require our most conscious attention in order to achieve the required balance.

Style, Comfort, and Competence

Another area where style seems to affect success is related to the idea that when we begin to feel uncomfortable in a situation, we may also begin to doubt our competence in that situation. If we equate discomfort with the idea that we may not be competent, we limit our success.

If our most comfortable operating style tends to be structure and detail oriented, we will probably feel most at ease in situations where we are organizing things, scheduling, working with time lines, preparing budgets, or doing research. With this style preference, if we must present information to a large group and there is expectation for humor or charisma, which is not our customary style, we may notice feelings of anxiety and then we may begin questioning our own competence. This happens because the presentation requires a different behavioral approach than naturally fits with our style. If left unexamined, this kind of discomfort could so severely limit us that it could impact on job performance, and perhaps even our health.

Along with the awareness that style is strongly connected to our comfort zone, it is also important to realize that we are capable of adapting our preferred style as necessary to fulfill the task and relationship obligations of our job. Keep in mind that it is not necessary to think in terms of changing a preferred and comfortable operating style. We only need to modify our style, on a situational basis, as necessary to enhance success. We also need to be aware that when we modify our style we may have feelings of discomfort, especially the first few times.

Style and Job Expectations

In the world of work, even volunteer work, those served have expectations about how the service should be delivered. If those expectations are not met, it is more difficult to win the approval or confidence of peers, clients or customers.

When discussing how style may align with success in a particular job, typical questions include: "Do certain jobs require specific operating styles?" and "As circumstances change, do the style requirements of the person in charge also need to change?"

Though the answers may seem simplistic, experience indicates that the "chemistry" that often exists between a candidate and those who will make the employment decision is, in part, based on a match between the perceived need for a particular approach and the perception of the style of the candidate.

Another reality is that once in the job, we have got to stay alert to changes in the environment. The style that helped get us get hired or gain favor could be the same style that contributes to loss of support if we can't assess needed changes and modify our style when it counts.

What is really important when considering if a particular style matches a job situation, is to look at the kinds of functions, duties, and expectations that exist. Then consider how much time is required in the various functions in order to be viewed as successful. Once the job is analyzed, consider how much time would require work that makes you uncomfortable. If the conclusion is that the amount of uncomfortable time can be dealt with, go ahead with the plan. If the conclusion is that too much time would be spent in discomfort, it might be wise to reassess the level of satisfaction available in day-to-day life. It is the daily ritual of doing the work that must receive attention. No matter how good the job looks from the outside, once involved, it is the daily reality that impacts satisfaction and enjoyment.

Focus of Communications

No matter where you go, if there are problems, you're likely to hear that communication is a significant issue. Whether affecting an individual, a team or an organization as a whole, the ability to communicate effectively is a constant concern.

Effective communication is a two-way process. The first half of the equation requires ability to effectively listen to others. The second factor includes the ability to self-disclose or confront in order to get issues on the table and still maintain a working relationship that fosters problem solving and planning.

Our style and the styles of those we associate with have a great impact on this process. Some styles more naturally attend to listening and support while others more easily confront and disclose. Knowing where a style tends to be naturally focused helps us to understand which parts of the communication process are easy and which are less comfortable and require more practice.

Task Management

There are so many systems available for managing time and task effectiveness that it is difficult to know which one to use. Common elements among many of these programs include ways to categorize activities and a variety of formats to help us keep better schedules and records.

Time management programs do not always acknowledge how personal style impacts our context for the whole idea of managing time and organizing work. For some, life seems too short to bother with a highly organized approach to how our day, week, year, or life should be structured. They believe things will take care of themselves as long as honest people are communicating and have good intentions. For others, style moves them to make meticulous schedules for both personal and professional time in order to be comfortable that they are achieving what is important in life.

If we can get a grip on where our style tends to lead us with regard to managing time and organizing work, we are in a position to make more conscious choices. Some of these choices may run contrary to our natural style, and may also increase our success potential.

Leadership & Management

Different organizations require different approaches to leadership and management, depending upon the circumstances that exist at a given time. There are times when an organization or a team may flourish under the leadership of a charismatic individual. There are other times when a hard-driving, task-focused approach may be necessary to the very survival of the organization. In still other phases of development, an organization or team may need a structured analytical approach or a laid-back, more mellow supportive influence that allows for healing and stabilization to take place. For a manager or leader to be successful, assessment and use of appropriate style, based upon current needs, is critical.

Maximizing Style

To maximize style, the first goal is to be familiar with the elements of our own style. This lets us know the kinds of circumstances where we will be the most comfortable and where many of our operating preferences come from. Second and equally important is to gain insight about the differences that exist among the people with whom we interact.

Exploring style helps us to better understand why some people seem naturally compatible while others seem to be at odds. It allows us to understand that there is no perfect style. Rather, each person's operating style brings with it some natural strength and some vulnerability. Strength can then be maximized and vulnerability can be offset by conscious personal choice

Style Assessment

If style becomes personal, as in, "I'm going to tell you what's wrong with yours," tension is immediate. How this issue is handled can dictate the emotional climate that must be worked through. No matter what approach is chosen, the process should be viewed as a "tool" that helps members find their place in the puzzle of a beautifully organized and effective team.

Observation and Feedback

One method that has been used to examine operating style is to observe the actions of others and then give them specific behavioral feedback directed at the improvement of their effectiveness. For this approach to be of value, observations must be strictly limited to behavior that is within the control of the individual being observed. This kind of feedback is often focused on what should be kept, deleted, enhanced, or changed.

The problem with this process is that it requires one human being to "objectively" evaluate the behavior of another and then give feedback in such a way that defensiveness does not block any positive information that can come from the process. In reality, this is very difficult to accomplish. The relationship that exists between the parties involved can become very intense. This happens because the person being observed is also making judgments about the observer. Often, the success of this feedback process pivots around the compatibility or incompatibility of the styles of the people involved. This may be especially true if those giving the behavioral feedback are not highly trained and practiced.

A typical difficulty in this process exists when an individual with a "General Patton" style is given feedback by one whose style is very people oriented. Quite possibly, without their awareness, the styles of the two people involved are so different that it is difficult for one to consider what the other has to say.

When a more dominant person is told to ask others for opinions before making decisions, it could be devalued if it comes from a person who asks others for opinions so often that he may be perceived as wishy-washy. As this example points out, feedback from one person to another often has as much to say about the person giving the feedback as it does about the person getting it.

Although this process can be effective, it must be carefully structured and monitored. Even with professionally trained facilitators, emotional reactions can be volatile and team members can go away thinking to themselves, "Who do they think they are telling me how I should act?"

Because it is difficult to find highly trained facilitators to conduct this kind of behavioral feedback, and because even with excellent facilitation there can be substantial resistance built up in the process; the use of diagnostic instrumentation may be preferred.

Use of Instrumentation

There are a variety of types of instrumentation that can be used to assess styles, behavior preferences, creativity, belief systems, flexibility, leadership, and almost anything else that might be desired. Some of these instruments are computerized and require the completion of an answer sheet that generates a profile. Others may be simple questionnaires that can be tabulated on the spot.

In addition to an awareness of what types of instrumentation are available, it's important to note that some instruments are supported by a research base while others, although still valuable as discussion starters, are not. Research-based instrumentation provides the opportunity for comparison with a "norm base" which can show how an individual's response pattern fits with a group of other respondents.

Self-Report Instrumentation - On this kind of instrument, the individual responds to a series of questions or sets of circum-stances. Tabulated scores result in an interpretation based on the individual's answers. The conclusions represent that individual's perceptions of the way he or she might behave or choose an action path.

One of the advantages of self-report instrumentation is that the result comes from direct input of the respondent and therefore may be more likely to be accepted. With instruments that have a strong research base, most people see results as being on target.

With instruments that are not built on a research base and are designed as discussion generators only, more variation may be found in the participants' receptivity to the results. This is not necessarily a problem. With this kind of an instrument it is the processing or discussion that takes place after results are generated that provide the learning.

Self-report instrumentation can provide positive and comforting information about one's operating style. It can also provide information that allows one to stretch and come to grips with areas that may be uncomfortable. All in all, self-report instrumentation represents lower risk in terms of generating negative group dynamics and defensive reactions than does a feedback structure that requires face-to-face input from others.

Peer-Report Instrumentation - Another option for assessing operating style is to use instrumentation that provides for the input of peers, colleagues, or clients. This type of instrument represents a slightly higher risk for personal discomfort than self-report instrumentation. In self-report instrumentation, individuals deal strictly with their own perception of how they might operate. In peer-report instrumentation, people are dealing with the perceptions of those who see them operate. When others are asked how someone operates, there is at least the outside chance that they may perceive an operating style differently than the person being assessed.

This possibility for differences in perception creates potential for a higher level of emotional response to results and inter-pretations. Sometimes, this type of instrumentation is designed so peers provide a perceived operating profile. Other variations of peer-report instrumentation allow for comparison of perceptions between an individual and selected others. This provides the opportunity to focus on the differences between a personal view and what colleagues or clients observe.

Choosing Instruments

Level of Risk - Because complicated dynamics can surface when using instruments that involve the input of others, self-report instruments may present the lowest emotional risk for participants. The self-report instrument usually generates less resistance and less emotional overload. For this reason, it may be the place to start in initial team building applications. As the team develops, and team members want an additional stretch; peer, client, or supervisor input into instrumentation fits nicely. When using peer or client report instrumentation, it is important to be prepared to deal with emotionally charged results, including denial.

Budget, Research, and Receptivity - There are many reasons for choosing specific types of instrumentation. Practicality of administration, research base, general "feel" or receptivity of results, and budget considerations come into play, to name just a few. The options range from complex, highly sophisticated and expensive instruments that can be used to analyze almost every aspect of an individual, team or organization to relatively simple inexpensive tools that serve only as discussion starters.

Viability over Time - One of the challenges in team training is to find instruments that present information in a format that can be kept alive in discussion as the team matures. For this to work, new information must be combined with data available from past instruments. This gives the opportunity to link information on topics such as leadership, flexibility, time management, diversity, beliefs, or listening. In this way, the volume of information available to the team keeps expanding.

Trust as an Issue - When used properly, instrumentation may help create an opening to build or rebuild trust. In rebuilding teams, it is frequently lost trust that must be reestablished before a team can reach maturity. Use of appropriate instrumentation seems to allow people to say to themselves, "Maybe some of our past problems have existed because we didn't understand these kinds of differences." Once this kind of opening has occurred, a team can move forward with a level of understanding that allows old baggage to be set aside.

Scope of Instrumentation

Starting with a general profile instrument establishes a foundation for a team to begin understanding why people may operate in predictable ways. It also provides a common language that can be used in team discussions. This is important because if the team is to have tools that make them more effective, each piece of information or each new skill should be something that is of real use. Among the sources for useful instrumentation of this kind is the Inscape Publishing Company (see reference section)

6

Belief Systems

It's tricky to break down the components that make us who we are without becoming overly simplistic or so complicated that practical application seems hopeless.

One way to do this is based upon a two-fold approach. In the previous chapter, the first element explored was the way we come across based on observable behavior. In addition to this, we must also figure out what might be going on inside a person's head as judgments are made about everything in personal and professional life. While a person's behavior style can be readily observed from the outside, the data base or belief system that is used as for making judgments is more elusive.

The Little Voice in My Head

The data that forms the basis of our belief system is composed of information collected through our life's experience and stored somewhere within our memory mechanism. This collection of information is what directs the little voice deep inside us as we decide the way things should be. Sometimes, that little voice is whispering so softly that we don't even realize that it is present. Other times, like when we back our car into a light post in a parking lot, it screams at us with its opinions about how dumb we are or what a stupid place that was to put a light pole.

Many of us are so unconscious about this little voice that when the idea is first introduced we may deny its existence. Further examination may show that it is this very same little voice telling us that no such voice exists.

The question is, "Are we willing to consider that there is some mechanism, sometimes subtle, and sometimes screaming in its attempts to help us judge what is right or wrong?" If so, then it is important to give some consideration to the origin, nature, and validity of information being used by that inner voice as it functions as judge and jury in our life.

A Computer-Based Analogy

In order to talk about our thinking processes in an understandable way, it's helpful to use some kind of a model or reference system. With the familiarity of technology in today's world, the computer works well as an operational metaphor.

In his books *What to Say When You Talk to Yourself and The Self Talk Solution,* Shad Helmstetter develops a model that suggests our brain operates much like a personal computer with a large volume of storage capacity ready to be programmed when we enter the world. The model further holds that the programming takes place through sensory inputs such as sight, hearing, feeling, and later, our own thoughts.

If you combine this idea with those of Morris Massey, author of *The People Puzzle* and a variety videotapes on the same subject, it is possible to consider how our thought processes are impacted by the generational influences we experience throughout life, particularly during our formative years.

In this process, we start with the premise that when we enter this world, much of the storage space in our personal computer has not yet been programmed. Since we know that there has been a continuing debate about the interaction of heredity and environment it seems acceptable to consider that some of the storage space in our personal computer may have already been programmed through heredity. Even so, there is still a vast amount of space available for the programming that takes place as a result of environmental influences.

Our first programming comes from our parents or those who we live with at the onset of life. In some homes that programming may be positive, supportive, and nurturing. In other homes that programming may be setting the stage for a debilitating thought process.

In the early stages of development, if we are told we are valued and loved and that we bring joy to life, those experiences become part of our personal storage files. If we are told that we have created nothing but problems since we arrived, those messages are also filed in our computer storage system. Combine this knowledge with the possibility that during our earliest years of life we may be incapable of evaluating the merit of these bits of input in any useful context. This tells of the special significance that those years take on in terms of the files we store.

To further the computer analogy, our storage files are continuously programmed in a logical progression by those with whom we come into contact as we move toward young adulthood. There is a recognizable logic to the way this happens. In addition to the influence of our parents, we may have close contact with extended family and friends of the family. What we see, hear, and feel from those people add to our files. For many, church or some spiritual structure may be next to be put in place. The structure and doctrine provided by religion can provide a strong next layer of file completion.

Coming closely on the heels of family and religion is the education experience. First come the things that we see, hear, and feel as a result of contact with teachers and other school personnel. As we continue with our educational experience, our files are expanded from contact with other students; particularly those we obviously dislike and those we like best. What they say to us, how they treat us, and whether we feel like we are a part of a group all provide input into our personal database.

As we move along in life, combinations of input from all aspects of our lives, especially those involving people who are significant to us, expand our files. What we see, what we are told, and how we feel as we interact with significant others (be they boyfriends, girlfriends, a role model we admire, or a person we detest) become part of our programming and food for our own thought processes. When we are old enough to think through the merit of the input which we have been exposed to, we can evaluate what makes sense and what does not

The Impact of Growing Up

With a basic understanding of this kind of programming, it is critical to think about the very nature of the information that comes to us through the process. Morris Massey suggests that much of the information that we take in is the result of circumstances specifically related to the generation in which we grow up.

Consider the difference in perspective between the person who was raised and "programmed" during one of the major world wars or depressions versus the programming of a person who grew up during or after the Vietnam War. The older generation would likely have received programming about how important it is for the country to stick together and because of scare resources, a "waste not want not" theme would be strongly impressed. In contrast, the later generation was more likely to have been impacted by the public controversy regarding decisions made by governmental officials. And perhaps as the economy became more stable, this generation may have also developed a greater interest in material possessions.

In earlier generations, people in the United States were likely programmed about the sanctity of marriage, the value of family, and the importance of loyalty to the country, the job, the union, or the team.

Later generations have received a very different message. The national divorce rate suggests that it's O.K. to terminate a relationship if things don't work out. Messages from media and advertising suggest that a person's goals should include the acquisition of as many material possessions as possible. The slogan appears to have become, "Whoever dies with the most toys wins."

In past generations, the message was that Mom should stay home and hold the family together while Dad went out to be the breadwinner. Today the message seems to be that both Mom and Dad can, and possibly should, be in the job market either to be sure that the family has everything it wants or to provide personal satisfaction and fulfillment. In the past, the message was that there were a limited number of professions appropriate for women. Today the message is that women can enter any profession they choose.

Evaluating Our Programming

It is important that each of us take a look at what life experience has provided and recognize that this program is now acting as a filter through which to view all reality and make judgments about everyone and everything.

It's a lot like a high-tech game where we put on a pair of goggles that are linked directly into a computer. When the game is activated, there is a sensation of being a part of the program. Our personal database operates much in the same way, like having a pair of eyeglasses plugged into our personal computer. Everything we see and experience gets run through those glasses or filters right into our personal files. Then we evaluate the experience based on what previous programming dictates.

This process of evaluating everything through our own set of filters is always with us. It is a natural and often unconscious process and many people are completely unaware that it exists. They not only don't know that it's happening but it also never occurs to them that their past experience may be their criterion for evaluating everything that comes across their path.

This programming can be so complete that it is easy to assume that whatever it is that "I" think must also be the natural viewpoint of others. The next jump can be to assume that if others do not share the same viewpoint, they must be missing something, not seeing the big picture, or not using common sense. Perhaps this is why the statement "it's only common sense" may not prove useful in sorting out sensitive situations.

Add to this the possibility that at least some, if not much, of the programming we received earlier in our life may be invalid in terms of today's reality. For some this is a scary concept. In fact, so scary that any suggestion that it should be examined is considered an attempt to take away some ultimate truth.

Specific Sources for Our Files

As we grow, we are bombarded with the political, social, family, and personal issues of the generation that produced us. This idea of being produced by a generation may seem odd. It may even be a turn-off. But, if we think about the differences that have existed during the upbringing of our acquaintances, we may not be surprised. Think of the difference between what our grandparents heard around the dinner table and what today's high school student hears.

If the environment that impacted the formation of our thought processes was one in which there was a great financial depression, we can expect to be carrying many beliefs that are based on the idea of scarce resources.

If we were produced by a generation where it was thought that marriages last forever and families stick together, today's divorce rate is probably very uncomfortable. If we were in elementary school during the First or Second World War, our beliefs about patriotism, loyalty, and government could be substantially different than if we were teenagers during the Vietnam War, wondering if our draft number or the one of someone we loved would come up next.

If family dinner table discussions were about the importance of "the union," to the survival of the family, gaining a decent wage, and for some, the attainment of life-or-death working conditions, it is likely that we still maintain some underlying beliefs rooted in our listening to those conversations. Likewise, if as children we sat around the table in a "management family" and heard adults talk about how unions would be the ruination of the country because they protected lazy workers and took away personal initiative, then we probably maintain some beliefs implanted as a result of those discussions. Whether around dinner tables, at family reunions, in church, at school, or with friends and acquaintances, our information files were subtly built and stored for use as background material to make decisions in today's world.

Assessing File Accuracy

The problem with our life file is that even when it was programmed, if we could have looked closely, there may have been questions about its accuracy.

If you doubt the contention that information stored from past experience could be erroneous, just look at issues related to race, ethnic background, and religious differences. It wasn't long ago that races were clearly segregated and many believed that this was the best approach. It wasn't long ago that people shuddered at the thought of dating or marrying a person from a different religion. Even today, these beliefs are the reasons for deaths in many countries around the world.

And what about political beliefs? I can remember, while in junior high school, having political debates with my neighbor. He believed that Stevenson should be president. He heard this from his parents who were Democrats. I believed that Eisenhower should be president. I knew this was true, because I heard this from my parents who were Republicans.

Many hours were spent arguing about Eisenhower and Stevenson. As it turned out, I won the argument because Eisenhower won the election. In reality, I didn't have a clue about what was really going on with Dwight Eisenhower or the Republican Party. I only know that what I heard from my parents and their friends greatly influenced what I thought. The political programming which I received as a young person was carried into my adult life. It was only after considerable life experience that I began serious analysis of what individual candidates from the various political parties were all about.

What's important here is that we become conscious of the information and ideas that are being used as reference points or "truths" when we make decisions. It is a difficult job to suspend the judgment that quickly comes to mind because of the experiences we have had in the past. Yet, it is a necessity that we at least hold off those judgments until we have heard the viewpoints of others and collected current data that can be used to support effective decision making and planning.

Cultural Awareness

As a semi-rural raised white male, one of my vast areas of ignorance was rooted in lack of multicultural or ethnic awareness. In the community where I grew up, I encountered mostly white Angelo-Saxon Protestants and Catholics. When I was in junior high school, if someone had asked me about major cultural forces in the world, I would have been hard-pressed to completely understand the question, let alone come up with an answer.

A Perspective on Diversity

My hunch is that as a young person, I probably related to the whole world as if it was made up of white people just like me. In school I had seen pictures of people from other cultures that dressed differently or had different skin color, but I had no clue about the implications related to those differences.

I suspect that many people have had similar experience. Their cultural programming may not have been the same as mine but it may very well have been as narrow in scope. Whether it's you or me, experiences we have had, if left unquestioned, represent programmed reference points as we consider today's problems.

With this kind of limited background, many of us started on a career path with a substantial disadvantage as we encountered diverse perspectives rooted in culture and ethnicity. To complicate things further, many people sincerely believe that if intent is pure and there is no desire to hurt anyone, any problem can be fairly resolved from their current perspective, regardless how narrow.

The fallacy of this assumption is that it is based on the premise that we can understand others whose culture or ethnic background is different than ours without understanding the life experience related to that dearly held culture or ethnicity.

Although we might never intentionally do something that would offend or cause conflict with others, we can be at a substantial disadvantage because of limited awareness. To make things more difficult, when confronted with the issue of becoming more culturally literate, groups of similarly programmed and well-intentioned people often respond by saying, "Why do we have to deal with this stuff? We don't have any problems here".

As this points up, previous programming can be so well entrenched that it blinds us to the needs and dearly-held values of others. If we expect to operate systems in an atmosphere that dignifies all, a broadened awareness is critical as a tool for teams as they do problem solving and planning.

Just Give Me the Facts

Many decisions appear to be factual in nature. In reality a large number of those decisions are not based on scientific facts but rather represent collected opinions, ideas, and belief systems. It is because of this that those with the most support can win the day and force a direction, which although popular, may not be the best decision available.

It's easy to add two plus two and arrive at the sum of four. The problem arises when the four represents dollars and we must decide how to divide them in a system where there never appears to be enough money to meet everyone's needs.

Recognize that in the process of sorting points of view and belief systems, people hold their own dearly. No matter how important our belief or point of view about an issue, it may run into conflict with dearly held viewpoints of others. The ability to manage the process of working through divergent viewpoints is where success or failure often shows up in leadership and relationships.

Dealing with deeply held views requires an understanding of their origin in us and in others. To do this we must develop listening and speaking skills. These are the tools that allow us to build relationships that facilitate dialogue, problem solving and planning.

To have a chance for success, we must be conscious of the basis for the decisions we make. We must acknowledge the beliefs we hold then suspend judgment while we listen. We must consider all points of view and seek out the sources of those viewpoints before we act. Finally, we must guard against the temptation to believe that we have been endowed with supreme intelligence, which funnels information to us that is irrefutable.

Flexibility

The previous discussion reminds us that there is no best operating style or belief system that makes someone an outstanding leader or guarantees successful relationships. If this is so, then what does contribute to the success factor? One view is that "flexibility" may be the key.

Flexibility can be viewed in several ways. One way is to think of it as a process that allows for movement, change, creativity, or variety in carrying a system forward. Another approach is to think of flexibility as it might show up in a wishy-washy leader who is unable to make decisions.

One view is to define flexibility as the ability to convey to others that what they think will be given as much consideration as what we think is important. If this is accomplished, others are more likely to commit talents and energies to a cooperative effort. In addition, this willingness to consider what is important to others also contributes to the perception that we know what they are doing.

To make this definition of flexibility a reality, it is helpful to use a structured process (including understanding belief systems, style, and specific communication skills) when assisting others, addressing conflict, gathering information, or working through problems.

Impact on Motivation

The reason for understanding this kind of information is so that we can help provide an environment within which people are motivated to work together. The more we know about ourselves and the more we know about what makes others tick, the better chance we have of creating such an environment.

For people to work together there must be an open, accepting atmosphere where each individual is valued and can feel comfortable about his or her contribution and relationship with others.

There is no factor more important than understanding the power of belief systems. It is this understanding that helps us to see why positions are held so dearly. It guides us to know where new information is needed in order to create the foundation for movement. And, it is the critical starting place in all planning and problem solving efforts.

7

Intangible Elements

Missing in most discussions about success is an examination of things that impact our decisions and yet are not necessarily concrete. This chapter attempts to quantify some of those key elements.

Much of the time we don't consider the idea that the potential success of any given endeavor is a probability. Probability implies that there are factors that can increase or decrease the possibility of our success. The more conscious we are about this, the more likely our decisions and plans can be rescued from the throws of chance.

The elements discussed here have surfaced, one by one, in different kinds of work and personal life situations. At first they may seem to be independent. Then, the more you think about them, the more they seem to be related.

As a composite, consideration of these elements seems important to insure a high probability for success. No matter what the situation or issue: a solution to a problem, crafting of a plan, or making a personal decision; careful consideration of these factors can help.

This idea has been explored in several discussion groups composed of successful people. Dialogue was interesting. One of the most important themes focused on how easy it is to move forward in very important arenas without assessing limitations.

General Areas to be Considered

Intangible components for consideration in decision making and planning include:

1. **KNOWLEDGE:** familiarity with facts, range of information, awareness, or understanding.

2. **EXPERIENCE:** a past personal relationship or direct involvement in processes needed to accomplish a goal…an event which has been lived through. Skill derived from practice.

3. **COMMITTMENT:** dedication or loyalty available to cause action to go forward under varying types of circumstances and levels of pressure.

4. **FEAR:** concern about risk, corresponding to the level of dread or fright existing within individuals or teams that may inhibit the ability to make forward progress.

5. **INTEGRITY:** power of character (honest, truthful, reliable, and upright) that can be sustained through the process.

6. **EMPATHY:** ability to put one's self into the shoes of another without being debilitated by the emotions involved.

7. **ORIGIONALITY**: being inventive, or creative; bring about something that has never occurred or existed before; not copied, fresh, new, and novel.

8. **CHANCE:** random occurrence, assumes that when luck is a factor, it can go either way. Statistically, chance could be half favorable and half unfavorable. In this scenario, anything we can't account for becomes a chance factor. It seems that chance will always be part of the game. The desire here is to be conscious of elements that impact success in order to lower probability of chance as a determining factor.

Scales for Specific Evaluation

To further explore the impact of these components a scale has been constructed for each. At first glance, the scales might be minimized. If viewed from a serious perspective, they can assist in achieving a more focused picture in reference to any problem or issue. If done with serious intention the scales do not always produce a feel-good result.

These scales can be used by individuals, or a group. They may serve as a focus tool in determining what additional provisions would increase your probability of success in any pending endeavor. They may also help when considering personal issues like job changes or professional advancement.

If nothing else, reading through these scales may cause one to wonder what does impact our ability to achieve personal goals and contribute to the lives of others. Perhaps, they may stir someone to come up with a better idea or a more sophisticated approach.

Directions for Completing Scales

Define the subject to be considered. Example: If the project involves changing a manufacturing process, or considering a personal promotion; each scale should be studied from that context.

Each scale has items numbered from zero to five. Read each item in the scale before choosing the one that best represents your status. Mark the chosen item and move to the next scale. Be aware of your reactions: comfort level, confidence, and confusion, as related to the response options.

KNOWLEDGE RATING SCALE

KNOWLEDGE: familiarity with facts, range of information, awareness, or understanding.

0. I know nothing about this topic/issue.

1. I have had casual conversations about the topic with friends

2. I have heard the opinions of professionals about the topic.

3. I know the views of a range of professionals and have done research on the subject.

4   I understand the views of knowledgeable people, have done specialty research and have identified patterns of information or knowledge.

5. I have complete subject knowledge; have studied a broad base of research & informed opinion. I know how the major parts fit together.

EXPERIENCE RATING SCALE

EXPERIENCE: a past personal relationship or direct involvement in processes needed to accomplish a goal...an event which has been lived through. Skill derived from practice.

0. I have been told that something is happening.

1   I have had a dialogue with people about how they have dealt with the issue & how it worked in real life.

2. I have observed the situation successfully dealt with & processed my observations with experts.

3. I have had experience with a related issue in "real life" or simulation and have processed my experience with notable authorities.

4. I have helped to deal with this kind of situation as the teammate of an experienced person(s).

5 I have had successful independent experience with this kind of issue while working from a broad base of prior experience.

COMMITMENT RATING SCALE

COMMITTMENT: dedication or loyalty available to cause action to go forward under varying types of circumstances and levels of pressure.

0. I do not know anything about commitment.

1. This may eventually be worthy of commitment.

2. I balance my commitments and could possibly fit this issue into my priorities.

3. I am committed with the understanding that there are a lot of things in my life to which I am committed.

4. I consider this an important issue. I am willing to be involved and to be clear with others about what level of responsibility I am willing to take as the issue moves forward.

5. This is one of the most important issues in my life at this time. I will give it all that is possible while keeping the rest of my life in balance.

FEAR RATING SCALE

FEAR: concern about risk, corresponding to the level of dread or fright existing within individuals or teams that may inhibit the ability to make forward progress.

0. I am scared and will not be able to function in any reliable manner.

1. I am anxious and may be able to function behind the scenes if supported & told what to do.

2. I am apprehensive but with support will be able to function as a contributor.

3. I will only be able to function outwardly in very low-pressure situations.

4. I am able to go ahead independently.

5. I have no concerns or anxiety about going ahead and can continue under foreseeable circumstances.

INTEGRITY RATING SCALE

INTEGRITY: power of character (honest, truthful, reliable, and upright) that can be sustained through the process.

0. I think I understand what integrity is.

1. I have, on occasion, thought about what is right or wrong in this situation.

2. I believe application of right and wrong can include consideration of self-interest as well as the interests of others.

3. I am aware of my self-interests and how they relate to the interests of others.

4. I balance my self-interest with the interests of others or the group.

5. I put the interests of other persons or the group ahead of my own when dealing with the issue.

EMPATHY RATING SCALE

EMPATHY: ability to put one's self into the shoes of another without being debilitated by the emotions involved.

0. I am not sure I understand the necessity for empathy in this situation.

1. To be successful you must remain unemotional, therefore empathy has no place in my mode of operations.

2. I believe emotions have no place in rational thinking and problem solving.

3. I don't need to walk a mile in another person's moccasins in order to understand him.

4. I can get a sense of the emotions of another and not be compromised.

5. I can sense what it must like for another person in a specific situation and use that sense to do a better job of no-lose problem solving.

ORIGINALITY RATING SCALE

ORIGINALITY: being inventive, or creative; bring about something that has never occurred or existed before; not copied, fresh, new, and novel.

0. I am not creative and cannot learn to be creative.

1. I have had ideas that created new directions and I knew where they came from.

2. I have had flashes of intuition that eventually were formed into an idea.

3. I have had ideas that were original and I did not know where they came from.

4. I have had ideas that created new direction and I was not aware of how they came together or where they came from.

5. I have frequently had new ideas that have no identifiable source. These ideas have often empowered new direction or solutions.

Is Anything Guaranteed

When these scales have been used in discussion groups, it was sometimes unnerving as participants came face to face with the idea that the success of our decisions is not guaranteed.

Realization such as this can be a great survival tool as we deal with important issues that face us in our careers and personal lives.

Tabulation and Scoring

Calculation of a composite score allows comparison using %100 as a basis for probability of success. There is no scale for chance. Chance is determined by what is left after you consider what you may be able to control. This is not a scientific score. However, it does tie intangibles together so they may be considered along with other aspects of decision making.

Category		Score
1	**Knowledge**	_____
2	**Experience**	_____
3	**Commitment**	_____
4	**Fear**	_____
5	**Integrity**	_____
6	**Empathy**	_____
7	**Creativity**	_____

Total 1 through 7 _____

Multiply Total above by 3 _____

Solution equals approximate % which may be under our control

Subtract % on line above from 100% _____

Solution is % that may be attributable to "Chance" uncontrolled. Chance is a 50/50 proposition

Analysis of Results

Don't go in with expectations about how processing should occur. Discuss or reflect on the results obtained. Sometimes, if the group does not get results they like, they will place their focus on discrediting the instrument. If this happens, just point out that the instrument is only to focus thinking. In any case, identify what is specifically needed to increase success probability. Remember that the value of this kind of activity is in its use as a personal reflection guide or discussion vehicle.

Debriefing

After you have studied each scale, jotted down your choices, come up with a score, and noted personal reactions to the questions, you enter a reflection phase. This process can be done on an individual basis; in dyads or triads; or groups. To encourage discussion, and reflection, here are some process questions to consider:

1. What were your reactions and feelings about each scale and the process in general?

2. What do you believe prompted your reactions to the ideas on these scales?

3. What resources or abilities exist for you as an individual or among team members?

4. What additional resources are needed and where or how can they be attained?

Make a Plan

Here is where the rubber hits the road. If an honest evaluation has been done, and deficiencies have been found, one choice is to ignore the findings because you were embarrassed, the other is to seriously look for ways to bolster areas of vulnerability.

If you choose to move forward thinking you will somehow know what to do and when to do it, you are relying on chance or perhaps intuition, to get you through. If you do this, remember that chance is always a fifty-fifty proposition. If you don't like the idea of chance calling the shots, seek the assistance you need.

8

Intuition and Gut Feelings

What if you have a gut feeling that tells you they're all-wrong? What if a hunch tells you to go a different way?

While some believe strongly in their intuition, others believe that they are completely rational… operating only from facts, and refusing to consider that intuition plays any part in their decision-making.

If you hold the latter belief, the question for you is, what mechanism does the evaluation of those facts and how large a role does it play?

A Rational Basis

In life settings, we often hear of rational processes for problem solving: lists to consider, steps to be taken, even scales to weigh factors involved in a decision. Yet, when it's all said and done, something within us says this is what makes sense. This is what adds up. This is intuition and it's at its strongest when hard science is scant, incomplete or non-conclusive.

Even solid science has a subjective element. This is born out in the scientific community with the acknowledgement that it is difficult to keep any experiment entirely pure. The reason is that the experimenter is thought to have an effect on the result of the experiment. This may show up in the way the experimenter chooses to set-up, observe, and evaluate during an experiment. These, combined with a personal bias about what might happen can make a difference in how the results of the experiment are interpreted.

Intuition and Reality

If positions taken by human beings have some effect on how a situation unfolds, then what our intuition tells us becomes even more significant. In this context, the idea of being a part of creating the reality we will experience is interesting to consider.

If our intuition can tap into others, as we talk to them, listen, do surveys… all seemingly concrete, or by some other, less definable, means, then intuition is a process that can impact practical reality. This can happen because intuition tips us off about when to back off, when to provide support, when and how to educate, as well as how to apply what we know to influence others.

The Reliability of Intuition

The answer to the question " is intuition reliable?" is told by the success of our decisions. The evaluation criteria used most are related to how well decisions fit into the "Zone of Acceptance" for the audience (s) being impacted.

From a practical standpoint, it's good to have maximum information available, on a conscious basis, while the intuition process is taking place. With this information you can be more confident that if conscious consideration is all you're getting, you are still on good footing. Anything else is a bonus.

A Structure to Work with Intuition

Mastering conscious use of intuition is easier if we understand some working definitions. Working definitions imply that there is a stated meaning for certain words as they appear in a particular context.

Because scientific methods available to clarify sources of intuition and evaluate its accuracy are in a state of infancy, it is likely that differences of opinion exist. This is not necessarily a problem as long as we spell out terms related to a discussion.

Listed below are some definitions that are helpful in understanding intuition:

Intuition: Knowledge obtained without rational though; innate or instinctive knowledge; immediate comprehension or cognition; "Knowing that you Know"; insight (seeing into a situation); discernment (ability to grasp what is obscure); realization (that may arrive at a seemingly magical moment), possibly after a long pondering of the problem. Intuition can also be expressed as a hunch or gut feeling.

Conscious Mind: The part of the mind that processes information... logical, organized, reasonable; focusing attention; perceiving or noticing with some controlled thought; aware (drawing inferences from one's experiences); the place where you think things through. (For more see Rowan)

Subconscious: The place where things "jell" usually without our awareness. The place; where information, opinion, facts, subtle signals, and rote memorization of formulas, charts, or actions, come together to yield the answer to a problem. All without our being aware that the process is taking place. In a practical sense, it allows us to type on a keyboard without looking at keys; it's "knowing" the answer to eight times eight; it allows us to play a musical instrument, or to flawlessly execute a Karate move under pressure.

Intention: Intention, as used with intuition, is a clarification of what you want to occur. When stating your intention, it seems to work best when formed as an answer sought or a problem to be resolved. Here you are not saying I want the problem solved in a specific way. You leave all options open so your intuitive process can explore a wide spectrum of opportunities. This is a different type of intention statement than when you state the intention to complete something in a specific way, once an initial path has been determined.

Open Intention Statement - An example of an open intention statement, when looking for general problem resolution or direction, might be something like this: *"My intention is (or I need) to find a solution to the budget problem in my organization"*. Modifications might include: " *I need to find a solution, or my part of a solution, or a starting point for a solution to the budget problem in my organization"*. When you form an intention statement, use your own words and remember to keep it open so you don't restrict your intuition as it does its work. You may attach a condition like... *which is fair to all concerned...* if you like. In any case, the evaluation of what you get can come later.

Closed Intention Statement - An intention statement directed at making something specific happen is different. In this case the statement could be something like this: " *My intention (goal or objective), based on information available today, is to balance the budget in our organization by reducing staff over a three year period via attrition, restructuring jobs, and without involving involuntary job loss.*" This is more the kind of statement that might be made after you have done all your work, including evaluation of your hunches, and arrived at an initial course of action. This kind of statement is very clear. It is also more closed to other options. The caution here is that even when such a statement has been formed, we should still remain open to other options we might encounter along the way.

Document Context - In the second example you'll notice the phrase *"based on information available today"*. It's a good idea to use this kind of language when taking positions. This provides a record of the information being used, where it comes from, and how solid it appears to be. You can also use a footnote system to spell out this kind of context in reports or written speeches. What this does is provide a more credible basis for evaluation of the decision or for future transition if circumstances change.

Ignition Point: Fire building requires generating enough friction to produce the heat to ignite a particular fuel source. The more susceptible a fuel source is to bursting into flame, the less effort is required to produce ignition. Ignition point also exists with people in terms of receptivity to ideas. In some situations, because of experiences they have had or the way they have been prepared, people are ready to receive and support certain ideas. Other times it may take time and work to spark their interest. Your timing, how your intuition has scored in the past, and the breadth of experience others have had, combine to determine how hard it will be to get ignition.

Where Intuition Takes Place

Conscious consideration is active thinking about a topic, issue, or problem while being aware of doing so. Subconscious processing happens without our awareness. Intuition can happen between conscious thoughts, in addition to conscious consideration and at times which seem to be totally separated from awareness of the topic or issue. Those times can include: when you sleep, eat lunch, and while driving, as well as while being stimulated in other ways… like off topic conversations, watching a movie, listening to music, attending inspiring lectures, or while exercising.

During these times we may have thought fragments, simple thoughts, streams of thoughts, even entire plans or solutions may arise. Whether a flash of intuition happens during a meeting or on the drive home, doesn't matter. Either can be helpful.

Because of the way these things occur, you have a strong sense that you "know" but you may not know how you know. The trick is not to tune out or intellectualize away these bits of knowing when they happen. Since intuitive bursts can fade quickly, its best to write them down or record them right away. It's impossible to know when intuitive thoughts will occur and they can slip away as fast as they come.

Often these bursts of insight hold up under scrutiny of peers during discussion. Sometimes these bits of knowing don't prove to be the answer. Even those that don't prove to be "the answer" often serve as a foundation that leads to a better decision. Occasionally, these "knowings" are completely shot down when held to scrutiny within a known zone of acceptance.

When an intuitive insight is shot down, you may want to hold off on the basis that the group or audience to be impacted is not ready for that particular hit on their reality. This does not mean that the idea will never be acceptable. Perhaps it requires another direction now while educating the audience for a different path later.

Enhancing Intuition

Enhance intuitive ability can be a big challenge. The ideas presented below give a quick summary. If you want more, there are volumes available.

Intention Focus: Requires only that the target or objective is clearly in focus while you go about your business, content that your intuition will work toward solution. Answers or partial answers may come at any time: when falling asleep, in dreams, as you abruptly awake in the middle of the night or as first thoughts in the morning.

Reflection: The process of reflection requires that we determine an intention and then allow our mind to contemplate, even wander, for a result, without obvious distractions. Preferably, this is done in a quiet setting where people are unlikely to disturb you. Some people lean back in their office chair. Others add soft music. Still others go to a favorite spot. Some like to hear birds singing, winds blowing, water rippling or waves crashing on a beach. The secret is not to have an agenda. Allow your mind to work with no expectations about results or how and when they may show up. For some, awareness will occur during the reflection, for others it may show up at a later time, often when least expected… like on the drive home, while exercising, or at a movie.

Prayer: With your intention clearly in mind, and according to your religious affiliation or spiritual beliefs, enter into a prayerful state and ask in the appropriate way for guidance that would allow you to serve in the best way. Again, answers may not be immediate.

Meditation: There are various methods of meditation. Most are looking for a way to relax the body and clear the mind of distracting thoughts. This allows higher-level thinking to occur... often without conscious awareness.

Binaural Beats: The binaural beat was patented as a tool to induce brain wave patterns that help us reflect, think, relax, and even increase creativity or intuition. Binaural beats are not recorded at a level that can be heard. The process involves sending one beat in the left ear and a different beat in the right ear. These beats combine to create desired brain wave states (For more see Monroe Institute). Several formats are available:

Natural Sounds – Involve use of waves or other nature sounds. The listener just leans back and listens to the soothing sounds. The binaural beat is not noticeable

Guided Imagery - Here, the beats are combined with soothing sounds and a voice to guide relaxation and focus direction. Again, the binaural beats cannot be heard.

Meta Music - This approach uses music as a vehicle for the binaural beat. Some selections combine with beats that help increase concentration. Others help with relaxation and encourage focus or creativity. Music compositions also vary to fit personal taste.

Most Important

Trust that your intuition and creativity are at work. Don't set up expectations about what, how or when things should happen.

No matter which approach you decide to use, follow your own path. Even if you choose to use guided imagery, if the instructions become cumbersome, go with your own lead. Remember, you have been doing fine up until now.

Curb expectations for startling changes and relax while your intuition works for you. Also pay attention to your environment, notice where you tend to get the best results. Is it when you are sitting, lying down, at the park, in the woods, on the lake, or while jogging?

Results of the Intuitive Effort

Results may be subtle to dramatic. Obviously, if the result of your chosen course provides you with a startling revelation, the process will seem valid. If it is subtle, even to the point that it seems nothing has occurred, the process is simply not over.

You may be startled by a very concrete thought that says, "do this" (sometimes really big, sometimes not). This could include an unexplained feeling that you need to talk to a particular person or to browse a particular bookshelf. You might even find yourself urged to attend a particular seminar, where – low-and-behold, a speaker... maybe one you were not planning to hear, says something that provides just what you need.

You may also find yourself befuddled because nothing clearly presents itself. The reality is that intuition will not be pressured. It has an agenda that won't be consciously manipulated. In some cases, it may take a form or present a message that you are not ready to acknowledge. You can do things that may encourage or support your intuitive process but it is unlikely that it will perform on demand to yield a result you dictate.

It's not that your intuition has abandoned you. It's more likely that, because of your psychological state, you are "jamming" the intuitive message and it can't get through. The more you use your intuition, the easier it may be for you to recognize its messages, even under pressure. A helpful thing to aid your intuition is to identify problems or situations early so that your intuition can work with less pressure, over time. Last minute crisis situations, dealt with during high stress, may not be the best place to say "intuition don't fail me now".

As Part of a Group

If your intuitive response is subtle, if you can't find a clear message, it can be very frustrating. If this is your common result you may even want to discount the whole idea as fruitless. If this occurs, don't give up. Remember, intuition most often gives you pieces or directs you to the next step. If you are a part of a team or a member of a group, its members may help you firm up ideas as you hear their insights. In fact, the reflections of the group and resulting discussions may provide the ignition point that solidifies your intuition into a position that may be stated or acted upon. This may then result in a direction that is supported by others or it may move the group to a higher level of thinking or performance.

On Your Own

If you are on your own, not part of a group or team, and your reflection yields unclear results, don't be discouraged. Just keep your intention focused on what you need to know and go about your daily affairs. While you do this, your intuition continues to percolate on the problem. This percolation can last for hours, days, weeks, months, even years (Yes, years. Think about those sudden unexpected insights about career changes or finding that perfect partner). This is why it's important to identify problems and goals early in order to allow as much time as possible to plan. You must trust that your conscious and unconscious mind have the capacity to work the problem out, to move you to the next level, or to point to the place where you need to go for help. You may even find part of your answer in a television program or radio broadcast you casually seek out.

Complementing Intuition

Help often centers on seeking people whose wisdom is respected and asking them open-ended questions. Once a question is asked, the goal is to listen. At best, this means resisting the temptation to dialogue until your source has had time to provide insight. Only after retrieving all that your source has or is willing to offer should dialogue begin. This dialogue includes careful use of self disclosure language (I-statements) followed by more careful listening... not the type of listening that focuses on what to say next... rather, the kind that seeks all the meaning possible.

Once sources of wisdom have been consulted, along with other information and data available, ideas may begin to solidify. Often the yield is more than one option or path. If the issue involves others, share these paths along with your perceptions about which one(s) to choose and what the consequences may be. If you are working alone, make a selection and remain open to feedback.

All through this process, it's important to remain open for reactions to proposals and choices. You can never be sure when the intuition process is finished. If you discover that your proposals are out of sync with the impacted audience(s), being open allows you to consider modification. Remember, one of your jobs is to find direction that will fit into the Zone of Acceptance that exists because of the belief systems of the audience(s) involved.

In "The Zone"

Being in "The Zone" (as differentiated from Zone of Acceptance) is a concept often discussed with regard to firing-line performance. This type of performance may be seen in an athletic event when a player makes just the right move at the precise time. It may also be seen when high stress or critical moments present the need for rapid-fire decisions to fix a problem or avoid a crisis.

In situations like these, there may appear to be no conscious thought. Just action. In other situations, several options may seem to appear from nowhere, in rapid fire succession. In these cases, conscious thought may occur as a choice is made among the options. Sometimes an outside opinion is quickly sought as the ultimate choice is considered. Other times the whole process is handled internally.

This form of being in The Zone is based on all that has come before. Your skills, your homework, as well as how past and present connections jell as required to deal with an important situation.

Risk Assessment

How much confidence should you have in your intuition? Having a strong sense that you know something is a sign that your intuition has been at work. The question is can you depend on that sense of knowing to be true or correct in your current situation? To evaluate this, you should consider doing a risk assessment.

Professional and personal risk is of concern too most everyone who is paying attention to the way today's world works. Some organizations have personnel on staff strictly for the purpose of assessing the level of risk involved in each activity considered. Individually, risk is also a big factor to consider when deciding how much we should push one of our ideas. Risk, personal, or professional, is a reality for all of us. We all face the issue of keeping enough chips in our pile. It is for this reason, assuming that survival is of interest, that our intuition, no matter how powerful it seems, must be considered with regard to how it will be filtered through the receptors (Zone of Acceptance) of those being impacted.

True Leadership

Don't get caught up in the idea, coming directly from your

belief system, that this is not the way real leaders operate. As a leader one of your jobs is to survive in the system. To accomplish this, it might be necessary to modify what your intuition says is "right" until you can educate your audience (community, team, clients, family, stakeholders, etc.) to the point that they can accept your ideas. The idea that I am right because I am in charge may not only be flat out wrong, it may cost dearly.

Presenting Results of Intuition

Accuracy is the guideword here. Avoid falling into the trap of projecting that you are the purveyor of absolute truth. Use precise language. This usually means I-statements (self disclosure language) to clearly show that you own what you speak rather than infer it is a representation of an all-knowing collective, sometimes called the infamous "They".

Using good self-disclosure language includes specifying when you are relating to data, opinions of others, experiences of self and others, consequences imagined, as well as your own intuition, hunches or gut feelings. A typical statement of this type may be constructed like: *"the data says... the opinions of staff seem to indicate... the financial situation is..., my prior experience with this kind of situation is..., and my hunch is that... or the options I see are...; what do you think?"*

This process of self-disclosure, listening to reactions, and considering insights of others, helps your intuitive system work. Eventually, this kind of dialogue and reflection yields a preferred path for a given time and place.

How People Respond

Fear of the unknown often prevents easy change. This fear may stem from one's personal concerns or from one's personal or professional programming that says that the new idea just doesn't fit.

From these kind of roadblocks come the challenge to either format the decision so it falls within the comfort zone of those impacted or to provide education and support so that comfort zones and belief systems can be expanded.

For some, any deviation from the current normal experience, even if he or she believes in an idea, can be a fearful thing. Only with support, over time, can these fears be overcome.

9

Foundation Skills

Talk to the coach of any sports team and she will tell you that success depends on how well each team member has mastered fundamental skills. In football, basic skills include learning to block, tackle, pass, run, and catch. Good football players are taught these basic techniques when they first start playing and they are constantly coached to refine their skills as they become mature players.

For the rest of us, training for success in real life should include: understanding of how people tick, knowing how to identify and diagnose problems, use of support and helping skills, ability to self-disclose or confront, and understanding that there are different kinds of planning and problem-solving procedures, one for value-laden situations, the other for tangible-based situations.

Psychologist Dr. Thomas Gordon has developed a skeleton to tie elements like these together. Gordon's approach has been long tested and retains its value because key structural elements are not affected by changing times. His approach uses cornerstone skills and problem-solving processes that have been developed and tested in counseling and organizational settings.

Fundamental skills

Here is an overview of basic concepts and activities that can be adopted as part of the foundation for a personal or team model. For more information find Thomas Gordon in the reference section.

Problem Analysis and Assignment

Problem analysis requires a fresh look to clarify the nature and magnitude of the problem as well as to establish responsibility for resolution.

Here you learn that it is possible for something to be no problem in one situation and a big deal in another. Consider this: in a work situation, can a two hour lunch be O.K. in one situation and not another? The answer lies in who it affects and how? Could one person think it's O.K. to spend two hours at lunch as long as the time was spent discussing business while another sees the same action as inappropriate at any time? Can someone then also assume that his interpretation is the only one that meets the requirements of common sense?

As circumstances become more complex or sensitive, problems can become nightmares if a clear method for analysis is not available. If a team member comes late to work or if a client questions a procedure, the decision becomes: what is the effect, who does the problem impact, what are the structural guidelines, and who has responsibility for problem resolution? The approach for clearly identifying a problem and determining the appropriate person to deal with it either moves the problem to an efficient resolution or mucks up the water.

In some organizations, the delegation of authority appears to be clearly addressed in organizational charts. Yet, there can be considerable lack of clarity about who actually has responsibility to take action as individual problems surface. And, when things go wrong, one may never be sure who might intervene. In this model, the preferred approach is for problems to be solved as close to the source as possible and by those who are most directly affected by the problem.

Developing Support and Helping Skills

To help identify the source of a problem, for deciding who is responsible for addressing it, and to work through the problem solving process; specific skills are available. These skills include how to listen in the same way a good counselor listens when helping someone sort out a problem. They also include how to interpret non-verbal behavior and use door-opening phrases such as "how does that work", or "tell me more" to suggest that you're listening and want to understand the other person's view.

Understanding characteristics of non-verbal behavior can help keep communication open. Folding arms across one's chest, the jutting out of one's chin or leaning back in a chair may make people question motives and perhaps cause them to resist telling you what's on their minds. Cooperation and trust may be enhanced by keeping arms loose and uncrossed, by leaning slightly forward, or by coming out from behind a desk rather than using it as a barrier.

For some, helping means giving advice and listening means thinking about what he will say next. While in school, most have been taught the basics of good English but not the specific listening and response skills necessary to support others when they are dealing with problems.

Self-Disclosure and Confrontation

In a problem situation, there are times when it is important for others to know what's on our mind. When those situations are less emotionally laden, the process can be thought of as self-disclosure. When emotions are high and issues are sensitive, that self-disclosure sometimes becomes a form of confrontation. Suppose a team member is always late to meetings but doesn't consider tardiness a problem. The situation must be confronted, and it must be done with as little negative impact as possible.

By being consciously aware of how self-disclosure works, we can identify confrontational situations, analyze the behavior at the root of the problem, and construct language to use in addressing the behavior. Usually, a three-part sentence is most effective. First, define the specific behavior; then point out the tangible effects caused by the behavior; and finally express your feelings related to the behavior. Example: "When you come late to the meeting (behavior), I either have to start the meeting over or take time to update you (tangible effect); that's very frustrating (or irritating) to me (feelings)". Of course, each person would choose words and tone that would be comfortable in this kind of situation. The significant thing here is that because we are using a specific model, we know that identification of three parts is important.

Behavior, Labels, and Language

Also important when working through problems is learning how to distinguish between behaviors and labels. Example: laziness is a label while coming to work late or not having work in by the specified time is behavior. Learning to construct language that addresses behavior and avoids labels helps keep relationships in tact.

As we experience our formal education, most of us are not taught to think in terms of dealing with specific behaviors and tangible effects. In addition, learning to carefully structure language to minimize negative impact is rarely considered.

Productive Dialogue

After you learn the skills for self-disclosure, and support, you can use the two skills together. After all, when you approach or confront someone about a problem, it is a natural reaction for the person to deny, resist, or become irritated.

These reactions can come from a person's surprise or embarrassment for not recognizing the problem himself. Or, he might just refuse to admit that a problem exists. That's why you shift from confronting to using listening skills. The switch to these skills helps convey that you want to understand and reach an agreeable solution. Productive dialogue requires that you shift back and forth, using helping or self-disclosure skills as necessary to dissect and clarify the issue.

Solving Problems

Once you know how to use skills for identifying, understanding, and exploring problems, the same skills are used in processing information and problem solving. The problem-solving process itself is very basic. By using skills discussed here, coupled with understanding personal style, belief systems, and how information is gathered, you make the process work. The basic steps for use in problem solving and planning are:

1. **Define** the problem & make sure everyone agrees.

2. **Identify** the criterion for a successful solution.

3. **Generate** a variety of possible solutions.

4. **Analyze** those alternatives.

5. **Choose** the most appropriate solution.

6. **Implement** the solution using a specific plan.

7. **Follow-Up** to see if the solution is working.

8. **Recycle** as necessary.

In Step 1, listening skills are particularly helpful in getting out all the components of the problem. Clear identification of the problem is the most critical step in getting an appropriate solution.

In Step 2, identify what factors must exist or what requirements must be met in order for a solution or plan to be successful. The general factors listed here should stimulate thinking. (For more, see Prigmore & Atherton)

- Is it compatible with contemporary expectations?
- Is it equitable and just (fair and impartial)?
- Is it compatible with important societal values?
- Is it politically acceptable?
- Is it legal?
- Does it satisfy relevant interest groups?
- Is it scientifically sound?
- Is it rational (per a problem solving process)?
- Is it efficient versus other alternatives?
- Is it workable (in practical application)?
- Does it generate bigger problems?

In Step 3, use the brainstorming process to identify possible solutions. Remember, even though it sometimes appears as if there is only one path available, **there is always more than one option**. Sometimes just a small variation in an idea or the combination of elements from several ideas ends up as the best available direction.

Brainstorming - In the brainstorming process, the maximum number of possible solutions is the goal. To accomplish this, participants' inhibitions about making suggestions must be reduced. No put-downs are allowed. Any suggestion must be considered, no matter how bizarre, and without belittling the person making the suggestion. This guideline is critical to making the concept work. When participants see that anything they suggest receives consideration, no matter how unusual it might seem, they'll begin offering more creative ideas To make this process most effective, it may be valuable to take a break after brainstorming is done. This break can be short, or it can be for a few days or weeks to allow reflection to take place. After reflection, even more ideas may pop up to be added to the list.

In Step 4, Examine the pluses and minuses of each idea generated. Each idea is evaluated based on available data as well as opinion. Again, allowing for reflection time prior to selection of the final option may be of value.

In Step 5, the best solution rises to the top of the pile and is formally chosen as a course of action. Use of consensus is the best choice here. Various types of straw voting may be of assistance in reaching consensus. Be cautious about moving to a quick vote that creates winners and losers. Those who lose often have resentment that ultimately works against desired goals.

Consensus itself is on a continuum. Even those who will support a decision may not be thrilled about doing so. Some groups go so far as to use a scale regarding level of consensus. One way to use this scale is to ask each person to indicate her level of commitment. Members can respond by showing 1, 2, 3, 4, or full open hand to signify where they stand. A closed hand indicates that we need to spend more time to get agreement on a specific point. Here is a sample continuum:

5. I'll support with enthusiasm and take a leadership role.
4. I'll work on committees and support the work of others.
3. I'll implement faithfully in my domain.
2. I'm not thoroughly convinced, but will give it a try.
1. I won't sabotage; and we must evaluate as we go along.
0. I can not buy in at this time. I will need more.

If a vote must be the deciding factor, keep working for a position that can get a very high percentage of the vote. A good goal would be 80 percent or higher.

In Step 6, we undertake the critical process of devising a carefully thought-out implementation plan. That's when the focus turns to the who, what, when, where, and how of the solution. Once the plan is devised, be sure to allow reflection time so that glitches may reveal themselves before execution.

In Step 7, recognize that you don't have to find a solution that lasts forever, just one that fits the current circumstances. Knowing this, build in a follow-up process for evaluating the solution and determining when it has grown stale.

In Step 8, the process is recycled at any time the solution runs into trouble and as many times as necessary to deal with the issue at hand. Remember that a glitch in the plan is nothing more than a new or unforeseen problem that needs to be solved.

Stages of Skill Mastery

Just as there are predictable stages in team development, there are also predictable stages that we go through as we learn new skills and concepts. Those stages are the same as ones we go through when we learn skills, like playing tennis, water skiing, or shifting an automobile's manual transmission.

People can literally be overwhelmed when trying to learn new skills. Getting a handle on these stages can help us understand why learning something new can be so frustrating and uncomfortable.

Blissful Ignorance

This is the starting point. This is when we're not yet aware of the new information or of how it will be to practice new skills and techniques. We don't yet have reason to be uncomfortable.

It might be like when we became old enough to drive a car and had to learn on a manual transmission. At first, it's all about what learning to drive can do for us. Then comes the realization that there are three pedals on the floor, and we only have two feet. Next, we realize that we only have two hands, and there are at least three things that we might be required to use them for. At this point, some of us even wonder how a human being can be expected to carry out all of these activities with only two arms and two legs. The irony here is that such thoughts may surface even though thousands of people are successful at the endeavor that is giving us trouble.

Now I'm Really Uncomfortable

When first introduced to new ideas and skills, even simple ones, many come to grips with the fact that they don't really understand how to use them. That awareness causes predictable discomfort. Based on a person's natural operating style, certain skills will come more naturally than others. For some, it is easier to pick up helping skills while with others it is more comfortable to learn self-disclosure or confrontation. The ones that fit best will be translated into action more quickly.

The discomfort experienced while learning these skills is as much a part of the natural learning process as it was the first time you learned to water ski, play tennis, do algebra, or speak a foreign language. It is in this stage that one may give up rather than take the time to practice or risk being embarrassed as rough spots get worked out.

I Think I've Got It

A third phase occurs when team members can apply concepts and skills, but that application takes concentration. In this stage, it's like learning to play golf or tennis. You've got to keep your eye on the ball and concentrate on the grip and swing you've been taught. In this phase of our learning, things often feel unnatural, uncomfortable, even forced. Likewise, when we use a newly acquired listening response, it may sound funny because it's an unfamiliar pattern. When the skill has not yet become an integral part of our language and our style, it can feel very odd, even though it may work just fine.

Smooth and Integrated

The final stage of learning is when once clumsy, difficult skills and concepts become automatic - and the language used is comfortable. In this stage of learning the skills and related concepts are so integrated that there is no longer a need to consciously think about them. They occur naturally as circumstances dictate. It's like jumping into your car, starting it, putting it in gear, letting out the clutch, pushing in the gas, turning on the turn signal, and rolling down the road without even a conscious awareness of what is happening.

Refinement

Much like when a seasoned athlete must learn new plays, some of these learning stages will recur again when a skill refinement is added. It might be like the small adjustment you made when switching from a four-speed to a five-speed manual shift in your car. You experience a few minor grinds but no big problem. In this context, it is good to consider that if no discomfort is ever felt, growth may not be taking place.

10

Agreement and Integrity

Agreements

As hard as it may be to believe, a big part of the success or failure of an organization (including families) is directly related to "agreements". Further, if three simple rules about agreements are followed, we have a lot better shot at staying out of trouble.

Rule One: Many people wander through their life experience not knowing for sure where they stand or what is expected. If you want to increase success potential, make agreements. Let people know what is expected and get clear about what others expect of you. If lack of clarity exists about the nature of an agreement, make a point to clarify it. If, based upon the behavior of others, you suspect that they may be unclear about the nature of your agreement, take the responsibility to clarify.

Rule Two: The second rule about agreement is, keep them. Too many people don't bother to make agreements, or they make an agreement and then the first time they experience some discomfort, they make independent decisions as if an agreement didn't exist. The best way to get in trouble with other people - short of not making agreements - is to make agreements and then ignore them. If you want to get into trouble with a board of directors, union, clients, support groups, staff, fellow members of a team, club, service organization, or your family, it's very easy - just don't make and keep agreements.

Rule Three: To keep your personal integrity intact, if you find it difficult to keep an agreement, go back and renegotiate.

Sometimes you will find yourself in a spot where it is difficult to renegotiate an agreement because a decision must be made immediately. If you have the option, put off the decision, even temporarily, while you renegotiate the agreement that is in jeopardy.

Hopefully, you'll get yourself into few situations where you're faced with a decision that will require you to deviate from an agreement. When it happens, manage the situation the best you can and then immediately get back to those whose agreement you have broken and explain the circumstances. Let them know why you had to break the agreement and why you could not come back to them to discuss it first.

If you have developed credibility, and if you have built up some chips because people know that you don't break agreements without an excellent reason, you have a good chance of maintaining your integrity.

A good way to keep agreements viable is to keep an eye out to the fringe of your operation, always looking for situations where a current agreement may not work well. In an athletic analogy, it's like being the great basketball player who can anticipate or visualize two moves or ball passes beyond the current action. This provides the opportunity to plan in advance and in anticipation of a changing environment.

Maintaining Integrity

Sometimes, we get in trouble about our agreements by telling ourselves that it wasn't in writing or it wasn't official and therefore it doesn't matter. The bottom line is, any agreement - written or verbal - is important. How we are perceived and how we carry out individual responsibility has a lot to do with personal integrity. That integrity will be riding on how we keep agreements.

If we don't manage our agreements we're no better than the center on the football team who decides not to block while the defense gets the quarterback. A football lineman who would act that way would soon lack integrity with his teammates. The importance of our agreements differs only in nature and execution.

Grinding Through Old Stuff

The debris that has built up among the members of some teams is so deep that the only way to move forward is to shovel it out. Sometimes, this shoveling process must be done in tandem with learning the new skills and concepts necessary to plan and problem-solve. Dealing with ill feelings and problems that have built up and caused bitterness, and mistrust, over many years is no small chore.

Part of the clean-up process involves clarifying roles and responsibilities. Another part involves keeping good enough records on current agreements and responsibilities that trust can begin to be rebuilt. People gain confidence with each other as they have more experiences with agreements that result in a no-lose situation for all involved. If you are a realist, you know that a win-win or no-lose approach won't always result in agreements that everybody is thrilled about. There can, however, be agreements that everybody recognizes as the best option for all involved even in a bad set of circumstances.

Really Deep Debris

If personal differences cannot be resolved fast enough, you may want to involve an outside facilitator who can use specific strategies designed to identify situations from the past that are getting in the way of forward motion.

If people are willing to get down to examining what it is that's getting in their way, some hurt feelings may come out - at least in the beginning. Knowing that emotions can run high and that feelings could be hurt during the clearing-out process, it is critical that your facilitator is skilled in working with group dynamics that may be emotionally charged.

It is also important that enough time is available to work through the issue(s) at hand and reach a stable point of understanding before ending the process. To be short the time needed to accomplish this can create an even more volatile and uncomfortable emotional climate. During this cleaning process some groups immediately recognize the importance of clearing out old stuff and complete the process with a sense of relief. In those cases, the group generally moves through the stage of conflict, mistrust, and emotion to achieve a very positive sense of team unity. Other times, team members may not be willing to risk putting their cards on the table. They will avoid issues. They will deny that problems exist. They will do anything to avoid emotional discomfort, and risk taking.

If this happens, the end of the process can leave you with an unsettled feeling. In such cases, it is not unusual to wonder if anything has been accomplished. In these kinds of situations, it's important to remember that feelings and emotions that are denied and buried may have been accumulated over a long period of bitterness and mistrust. When people have been hurt and are afraid that it could happen again, time must be allotted for them to see how things will work in the future.

People move through this stage of development much like a student progresses while learning to read. Simply speaking, if a student is in book two, it's only realistic to expect that it will take some time to get into book twelve.

Constructing a Playbook

Laws, policy, and operational guidelines, are no more than formalized agreements. They spell out processes and procedures that will be used to deal with specific kinds of issues. They represent prior planning. The only difference between planning and problem solving may be that planning takes place before the event, while problem solving takes place when the event is upon us and may be accompanied by a more highly charged emotional environment.

Formalized plans that have been developed and agreements that have been reached form the playbook for operation. Wise people are always looking to the edges or boundaries of their operation to see what's coming next. This allows for review of plans or agreements and allows time to develop new ones that keep ahead of potential trouble.

Inclusion and Camaraderie

How to develop and maintain relationships can seem like a mystery. It means that something more than an official or required connection exists. Some call this a sense of inclusion. It develops as people work together in an atmosphere that honors and respects each person. It grows as success grows.

If there is a small number involved, it may be easier to facilitate the bonding process than if there are twenty, forty, sixty or more, but make no mistake, relationships that are developed are part of the foundation for success.

On the football team where members like each other, the lineman who is outmatched and overpowered is more likely to get help from his teammates than a lineman in the same position on a team that does not get along. The idea that I'll do my job and I don't care what others do won't fly when things get tough. It reminds me of the story my father told me about the halfback who did so much bragging about his personal prowess that the linemen got together and decided to see how well it worked for him if they stopped blocking. You know the moral of that story.

This is not to infer that everyone who must interact together must love each other. In some cases, a pleasant working relationship is the appropriate goal. Such a relationship means people can interact in a relatively comfortable environment most of the time without sniping at each other. It means avoiding opportunities to criticize others. And perhaps most importantly, it means getting the issues on the table to be discussed on their merits.

Avoid the Set-Up

Some people set themselves up by fantasizing that it is realistic to expect to eliminate all problems. The fantasy continues with the belief that once done, life will then move forward effortlessly. This is the ultimate set-up whether it is in personal or professional life.

The set-up comes from believing that there will be a point in life when there won't be any more problems. In reality, as you develop a structured approach for dealing with problems, you'll soon recognize that whenever a current problem is eliminated, another set of circumstances occurs and a different set of problems appear or move into priority position. For this reason, our focus must be on developing a problem-solving system.

Ultimately, we can come to think of ourselves as a problem-solving mechanism; constantly on the lookout for new problems, and then putting our machine in motion before damage can be done. The goal of the machine must be that when one problem is solved, a bigger one is not created. That's an important rule of thumb when evaluating solutions to present problems. If a problem has been solved and a bigger one has not been created, then progress has been made.

11

Maximizing Talent

In a new situation, a first priority is to analyze past history. This is done to determine what is valued as well as what has been counterproductive. This kind of analysis must be continuous.

Every major activity should include some kind of debriefing, where both pluses and minuses are noted. Using the three questions: "What I like," "What I would like to have done differently," and "What needs attention the next time," are good starters for a debriefing session.

Evaluation should not be about comfort or how much we "liked" the content or situation. If we are to keep moving in difficult times, we will often face uncomfortable situations and we will be constantly challenged to learn new things, even if uncomfortable.

Follow the Playbook

Make it part of routine operation to discuss and evaluate how well the playbook is being followed. Consider how well people are living up to the agreements, policies, or procedures that have been established. If problems exist, reevaluate the nature of agreements and make adjustments.

If agreements are being ignored, recycle the problem through the problem-solving process to determine what must be done to make things work. Ignoring your playbook can be just as destructive as it could be for a football team during the Saturday game.

Continuous Evaluation

When working with a group, one continuous job is to identify the strengths of individual members as well as the strengths of the group of the unit. In any given year, a good coach who doesn't have the luxury of hand-selecting personnel will make modifications in offense, defense, and play selection based on the strengths of the team's players. If a quarterback can't throw or ends can't catch, it's smart to modify the game plan to minimize reliance on a passing attack.

The same is true for the rest of us. We must know the nature and sophistication of our own skills and those possessed by each member of the team. Some people may be excellent promoters, others negotiators, still others may be great detail analysts. Some may be excellent public speakers, while others possess unusual intuition. You might also notice that some are stronger under pressure and in conflict situations.

While the ultimate goal is to elevate the skills of each team member, it is also important to allow team members to work from their strength as much as possible. This means that members who are strong at detail analysis and situational intuition might be the ones you'd want to assign to a financial planning team. On the other hand, those who are natural promoters or possess the ability to inspire others are the ones to consider for work with staff and client relations. Certainly, when the going gets tough, and you can't afford to let them see you sweat, you'd be smart to call up those who maintain their cool under pressure.

The boundaries of this kind of assessment are broad. They can even include such things as an analysis of how your team members dress and manage personal appearance. A team probably wouldn't want to be represented at an important meeting by the member who prides himself on his collection of funny ties and bright plaid pants.

Although differences can be subtle or dramatic, the overall success of the team is partly dependent upon using the current strengths of its members. At the same time, the team must provide opportunities for members to stretch and try out skills that they need to further develop. In short, the systematic approach to getting the maximum impact is to utilize the strength of members, identify their areas of vulnerability, and then make plans to minimize exposure in areas where skill development or concept mastery is not yet up to par.

Beware of the Moving Target

One big trap for a team is to fall prey to the assumption that once a plan is made it should be followed regardless of the consequences. It's important to realize that sometimes the best-laid plans begin to fail under fire. This recognition may be the difference between success and failure.

Even with the best planning and consideration, which includes all available data, there will be circumstances when plans will begin to show frailty soon after implementation. When this happens, regroup, identify glitches, and change direction if needed. This is no different than when a basketball coach makes adjust-ments at halftime or when the captain makes instant changes on the court because of the way another team sets up its defense. A good task team makes provision for its own halftime discussions and in-game changes in order to insure the best chance for success.

Player Accountability

There must be an expectation that each player will be held accountable. That accountability can take the form of expectation that each team member will participate and contribute fully in all activities.

If team members are not carrying out their responsibilities, conversations should be held with them individually or the issues should be discussed with the group as a whole. The skills and problem-solving process which team members have learned are the very tools that can enable the team to solve its own problems. To keep the team viable, members have a responsibility to use their self-disclosure and confrontation skills to identify behaviors that are not supportive of the team's goals.

In the world of the professional athlete, if the quarterback decides not to carry out diversionary activities before handing the ball to a running back and that running back gets crushed, you can bet there will be a discussion among the team members. If you find lack of participation or cooperation to be a big concern even after team members have had skill training and development experiences, it may be wise to bring in an outside consultant or facilitator to help the team deal with that specific problem.

Player Development

Expecting too much too fast can create an atmosphere that threatens group members and closes down interaction. Time is required for the integration of skills and ideas newly taught or conceived. Stay attuned to the verbal and non-verbal cues that tip you off when it is time to back off and give some space. Even highly-skilled and knowledgeable people will need time to find their place on a new team, a team that is being reorganized, or a team that has new players. Having a plan for identifying and integrating new team members can do a lot to keep things running smoothly.

Backup and Utility Players

Being on the lookout for backup players is important to success. Inevitably, team members will be lost. Part of the success of team leaders will depend upon their ability to think ahead and develop those who can fill key positions on a permanent or temporary basis.

One of the things that can be done to develop good backup players is to develop good utility players. That means giving members the opportunity to operate outside of their usual niche so they can develop a better understanding of the big picture and show their growth potential.

One strategy used to develop that potential is to involve every team member in some responsibility that requires thinking as well as interaction beyond his or her typical job or frame of reference. At first thought, some might balk at the idea of this kind of expanded expectation. However, if these kinds of opportunities are presented with an awareness of workload pressures that already exist, the results can be positive both for the organization and the individual.

A Feeder System from Within

To mange ever-present player turnover, a feeder system should be developed.

Developing a feeder system means nothing more than looking at available opportunities that exist within the organization and then provide candidates the opportunity to participate. It can include conducting activities that facilitate the trying on of new hats in controlled moderate risk situations.

If you combine real-life opportunities with training programs that allow people to enhance their leadership skills, you have the makings of a feeder system.

Attracting Talent from Outside

Even with an excellent feeder system, there will be times when you need an outside candidate to fill a particular position. This may be because of special technical requirements or needed skill in human relations. In these instances, the reputation of a team may be a key factor to what kind of talent can be attracted.

With the sometimes devastating pressure that exists for many of today's organizations, the knowledge that one is working on a team that will provide support and which works together to solve problems can be a great comfort.

Titles versus Functions

As teams work together, their ability to identify, diagnose, and solve problems depends on their ability to rely upon the strengths of every individual on the team. There must be a spirit of cooperation and willingness to do what is necessary.

This kind of mind-set means that getting the job done is more important than titles or position. It means that in a truly creative problem-solving session, members might end up doing something that their colleagues in other systems might think is not part of their job.

Establishing Boundaries

Each person on the team must be given reasonable freedom to run his or her own show. This means freedom to operate within a set of pre-arranged agreements. The idea of running one's own show within agreed upon boundaries brings up questions. "Are you really running your own show if you have boundaries?" The answer here is that everyone has boundaries. Everyone operates within an area surrounded by restrictions.

If we pretend, even for a moment, that there are no boundaries or that each person should establish the boundaries as he or she sees fit, then that particular part of the operation is running in a vacuum and someone is eventually likely to get nailed. The real question is, "Can clear, workable, operational boundaries and agreements be established?"

When trouble exists over this issue, it is generally not because agreements can't be reached but rather because not enough time and commitment have been put into reaching them. Well thought out plans, policies, procedures, and agreements often represent the boundaries within which an individual must operate. In this perspective, it is completely acceptable, while operating under a current agreement, to continue discussion, negotiation, and attempts for revision. At the same time, barring moral or legal factors, it is unacceptable to second-guess a team member who is operating in accordance with an existing agreement, and it is unacceptable to ignore a current agreement.

Trouble Spots

Being promoted to a new position and having the responsibility to supervise a position previously held can be particularly troublesome. There may be increased temptation to step in and straighten things out. And, the longer the time spent in the position and the more successful the experience, the more likely the temptation to become overly involved.

But, "What if there is a disaster in the making?" Surely that is a good reason to wade in without guilt. The answer to that question is simple. Go to the person who is now in charge. In a collegial fashion that one would expect from a supportive teammate, give that person the benefit of your perspective. Use the skills you have learned. Be willing to present your perspective in the form of "tips" that may be of help. Be willing to engage in dialogue (using your support and disclosure skills) to lower resistance to your ideas. Finally, recognize that the person who is now in charge is the one who is sitting on that particular dynamite keg.

If the fallout will land in your territory, attempt to do no-lose problem-solving using the skills and structure that you both understand. Only resort to use of a power position if you don't get cooperation in the problem-solving process. If the team has been functional in the past, you have good odds of working things out without being perceived as the invader of another's turf.

On more than one occasion, you may face discomfort when a teammate makes a different decision than you might in the same situation. Here, its important to remind yourself that as long as the decisions were within an agreed-upon framework, the limit of your intervention might best be to influence by making suggestions for consideration. Sometimes this could mean engaging in a dialogue to insure that boundaries are in place and factors thought pertinent, are being considered.

At this point, it's anyone's guess as to whose decision would be best. And, on good teams it's the privilege of the one in charge of a particular arena to call the shots and be responsible for the consequences. If consequences of a decision are significant in either a positive or negative sense, a debriefing should be held so that what has been experienced can be translated into learning for future circumstances. The debriefing processes may be no more than conversations focused on what was done, what outcomes were observed, what was positive, and what could be done better in the future.

Rookies

One of the biggest contributors to failure of new team members or members who have moved to new positions does not rest in their technical competence or proficiency. Rather, it stems from an inappropriate focus or a lack of understanding of either the formal or informal structure that they must work within.

In the big leagues, the first year of experience is often called the rookie year. It is given a special designation because everyone knows it is a critical year in the making of a successful player. If the player gets the right guidance, he or she has a better chance for success. To insure that success, the coaches and the other players on the team maintain a special awareness about the presence of a rookie or a new team member.

Mentoring

Many times, all it takes to increase success probability is to consciously link a successful experienced team member and a rookie with the expectation that interaction will take place. Sometimes, it is necessary to establish a structure for the mentor arrangement to work. This structure can be loose or it can be so specific as to lay out dates and discussion topics that correspond to the times during the year when important or sensitive job functions must be completed. The minimum requirements to insure success in a mentor relationship include openness from both parties and accessibility of the mentor to the new team member. If either of these elements is missing the process might as well be non-existent.

12

A Better Game Plan

You may have heard the saying you're no better than your next time out. That's probably true. No matter how many good things have happened in the past, judgments made in the future will depend upon future performance. Of course there may be chips built up from past successes but without the ability to continue to overcome obstacles those chips will fast dissipate. Understanding this reality and knowing that change is taking place at an incredible pace should be enough to keep us on a constant search for better options and a better way to do things.

Scout the Opposition

There will always be some opposition to the goals that you want to achieve. Opposition can come from within, or from the external environment. Although an opposing point of view does not have to be accepted, it's got to be understood if there is to be a chance to move through it to accomplish a goal. The best coaches and players know that the better they understand their opponents, the better chance they have to win the contest.

Organized Practices

Think of every gathering you have and every meeting you hold as a practice session. In practice, new situations are analyzed, status of players is assessed, problems are identified, strategies are devised, and basic skills and operating structure are reinforced.

There are many books written on how to run an effective meeting. Most talk about making every minute count. But, just because we know the importance of an efficient well-organized practice does not mean that every minute must be spent hammering out plans for task accomplishment. On a good team, time is made available for comradeship. Activities can include those intended to enhance team relations and inspire intrinsic motivation.

Changes in the League

Staying in touch with changes in the league means having scouts who can provide insight about what's coming long before it hits home turf. It means actively monitoring both formal and informal channels of well-versed opinion. It entails looking for ways to influence outcomes while flexibility still exists. It also necessitates building strategies to keep stakeholders informed about what's coming and how your organization will be impacted.

The best way to appear as though your act is together in a changing environment is to predict issues ahead of time. Then, explain why change is happening and lay out a plan that can be seen as a smart way to keep your organization on the right track.

Dress Rehearsals

The night before the football game at most local high schools, the team is out on the field doing a walk-through of the next day's strategy. The goal of these dress rehearsals is to insure that the game plan is executed with a smooth fluid style where each team member knows his job and all possible hitches or loopholes are identified and eliminated.

Whether a new program, product release, budget proposal, or a presentation of the newest sales strategy, the success of delivery is as critical as the performance of any athletic team. A dress rehearsal with a selected audience of colleagues, clients, or consumers can provide the opportunity to clarify complex or confusing statements, charts, or handouts. It also provides experience with answering questions that will inevitably arise in the big game.

The value of the dress rehearsal is easy to underestimate. Yet, inevitably it provides valuable information. At a dress rehearsal, don't let those on a team get by with partial presentations or statements like, "I'll probably present this as a chart" or "I'll probably use a handout here." It's important that every chart and every handout be complete (at least in draft form) for the dress rehearsal. This is the only way that the glitches will be found and the tricky questions uncovered.

If you find it impossible to organize a dress rehearsal, try visualizing the event as it may occur. Go through each step. Including hits you believe might be coming your way. Picture worst-case scenarios and visualize specifically how you will react to them. Include how you will look, and what you will say. This process can help take the sting out of a situation what may be fraught with pitfalls and disagreements.

Don't forget to practice your listening skills, self-disclosure language, and problem solving approaches in the visualization. The closer you can come to the potential reality, the more helpful the visual rehearsal will be. If the situation has potential to be rough on you or if you expect emotions to be high, run through the visualization until you can complete it with confidence

Listen to the Players

Just like big time coaches, we have got to recognize that we have talented players out there in the trenches. The people on the team's front lines know what it's like to fight the battle every day. They know who is beating them up and what they can handle. They know where their skills are working, when they're being double-teamed, what will work easily, and where they are likely to get blown out of the water. In short, your players know the opposition on their battlefield. Listening to and understanding both the tangible parts of a problem and the emotional aspects are the first steps in the improvement of any situation.

Willingness to listen does not mean that the status quo or ineffective solutions must be accepted. Through mutual needs problem-solving, teammates can wrestle to find the best approach to a current situation. Listening validates team members as professionals, conveys support for them, and lays the foundation for effective problem solving.

Players Won't Always Be Happy

Determining the satisfaction level of team members can be tricky. There is a difference between being happy in a fanciful way and being satisfied that the team has developed an appropriate process for working together.

Teams that deal with real-life problems contend with differences in personality, and deal with dearly held value and belief systems can't help but encounter situations where some are going to be unhappy. Sometimes, discomfort exists because someone will insist that certain viewpoints get consideration even though they may not lead to comfortable solutions. Other times, team members may believe that too much position power was used. On still other occasions, unhappiness can exist due to the grating of one personality type on another as the team agonizes for hours in an attempt to bring forth a "miracle-like" decision.

For the team to continue to be effective, the players must recognize that there will be times when they will be unhappy or at least uncomfortable. At such times, effectiveness may lie in the team's willingness to process their feelings, individually or in a group, and to participate in team maintenance activities, which foster relationships that help the team survive under pressure.

Popularity of the Coach

Sometimes, the coach or captain is in a difficult position because of being held responsible for specific outcomes that are non-negotiable. When this circumstance exists, the coach or captain may be seen to have different needs than other team members. When this occurs, it's best to present the non-negotiable factors and try to get the team to understand why they exist and where they come from. This can be difficult if team members cannot understand the logic that is being imposed or legislated.

Even with best efforts, team leaders shouldn't expect that every issue brought to the table will be accepted with open arms. Also unrealistic is for other players on the team to expect the coach to be able to control the team's agenda to eliminate all unpleasantness. Don't fall into the trap of thinking that to have a good team, everything must always feel good to all concerned.

Empowering Your Team

It's easier to bring the team together for its first experience than it is to keep energy and commitment at peak performance level over the long haul. When teammates have their first training together, it can be both enjoyable and inspirational. People often walk away from this initial experience thinking that they have what it takes to beat the giant. Then, the day-to-day list of mundane grief that invades the life of today's leaders and problem solvers begins to drain energy and allow team members to drift apart.

To keep a team vibrant requires a constant search for ways to re-energize commitment. One approach is to run workshops or daylong events designed specifically to energize teams. Put together events that require team members to get together in an atmosphere that is not overwhelmed by the day's problems. Sometimes a simple morning breakfast session can help reinforce the value of the team effort. Other times, an entertaining or inspirational speaker will work.

Whatever the methods, be sure that specific acknowledgment of the contributions of the team and individuals on the team are celebrated. Be sure that team members never lose sight of the success attained as a result of their joint efforts. Reinforce the idea that the success of every individual on the team is possible because of the support that has existed among team members. When acknowledging teammates, choose words carefully and don't be afraid to express emotion.

In Touch with the Owners

Anyone who follows professional teams or enjoys an excellent symphony orchestra can see that the surest way for a coach, conductor, or key performer to lose his job is not to focus on the values of the owners and patrons of the franchise. Even highly successful individuals have left their positions under the guise of seeking expanded opportunities when insiders knew that the separation was because they lost contact with what was important to the owners. Sometimes, they lost touch with the image that the owner wanted to project. Other times, the individual's operating style was in conflict with the values or belief system of the owners.

What Works

Even with a strong belief in at least a quasi-scientific approach, it's important to know that a success key is to "do what works." This means, barring legal or ethical problems, use the idea that will get the job done with the least negative backlash. This requires being open to ideas from any source. It doesn't require a philosophical, religious, or interpersonal relationship, let alone complete agreement with the originator of the idea. Even a strange idea presented by someone who is not your favorite person may be just the ticket.

13

Constant Improvement

When the football team lines up over the ball, the positioning of each player is crucial. As the quarterback calls the signals, each player receives keys or codes that direct and time player action. When the ball is finally snapped, all players must be moving in synchronicity or the effort will be less than fully successful. Each player must carry his weight individually, and each player's individual effort must be coordinated with that of the other players.

Likewise, effective work teams require the development of a clear framework for operations. It is important to know about style and belief systems as well as basic skills that form the backbone of such a system. You've got to clear out old debris, make plans, and keep agreements. Together, these elements might be thought of as fundamentals.

No team can operate as a smooth functioning unit if the fundamentals are not in place. But that is not the end of it; once the fundamentals have been taught, the next step is to practice. The goal here is to refine skills by practicing in real or life-like circumstances.

Practice Formats

The same kind of logic that applies to an athletic team applies to us. We will not become good listeners unless they have an opportunity to practice listening skills and receive feedback that can be used for improvement. Likewise, a system to improve self-disclosure, confrontation, problem solving, and planning skills is also necessary.

Small Group Discussion

Small group discussion can be a great tool for asking questions about new skills, sharing of opinions, evaluating data, exploring values and beliefs, brainstorming, and the like. When deciding how many people to include in a small group, keep in mind that as the group gets larger, full participation of all members tends to be reduced.

A group of four to ten people is a good general guideline. Adjustments can be made based on observation of participation levels. This size range allows the group to be self-directed, yet when specific assignments are given, to be responsible for arriving at assigned outcomes. If left to its own means, the small group can be a relatively safe environment because group members can select their own level of participation. Members are not generally asked to practice skills or disclose information beyond their personal comfort level. This is perhaps the most comfortable kind of group activity.

Dyads or Triads

Once a skill has been presented and demonstrated, participants can pair up in "dyads" to practice by using a non-threatening problem or situation. In this kind of practice, each member of the dyad takes a turn at using new skills, while the other member presents a real or simulated problem. After the skill practice is completed, each person discusses with the other his or her perception of how the activity went and how the new skills were utilized.

A slight variation of this approach involves adding a third person to the group. In triads, a new opportunity exists. In a three-round rotation, each person has the opportunity to practice his or her skill, to know what it's like to be on the receiving end of the skill and to observe an interaction where the skill is being applied.

The big advantage of the triad is that the observer can often give a different perspective than either of the two involved in the actual practice session. This is because the observer is not concerned with practicing the skill, or presenting the real or simulated problem. This removes the observer from the emotional climate generated by the actual problem being considered as well as the learning stage that participants are experiencing.

Group Simulation

Structured groups allow members to practice activities that involve the assignment of various "roles". Each member is responsible to carry out his or her real or simulated role in order to experience a variety of possible exchanges and consequences.

During this kind of activity, the facilitator or trainer may periodically interrupt the activity to discuss how the various roles are interacting. An activity of this type might involve assigning roles that are anticipated in situations that may be encountered. Some of these roles can be productive and some destructive. In this environment we gain first-hand experience of what makes things work and what gets in the way.

Audio or Visual Recording

A more sophisticated and sometimes more threatening activity includes use of audio or visual recording as a learning enhancement. Audio recording tends to be slightly less threatening than visual recording, because there is less to be observed or scrutinized.

Utilizing audio and visual recording makes it easier to understand what behavior interactions have occurred. They also provide for a rerun of the process after cognitive and emotional overload have receded.

For this kind of activity to be successful, an appropriate atmosphere must exist. The group must be open, accepting, and supportive in the process.

Processing and Debriefing

An integral part of all these activities is the aspect of processing or debriefing. Anytime we are put into a situation to practice new skills, sort new information, plan, or solve problems, some time should be allotted to talk about what happened during the session.

Sometimes interrupting during an actual discussion facilitates this processing or debriefing. This gives participants the opportunity to reflect on immediate circumstances. Other times, the processing or debriefing takes place at the end of the activity.

Another good operational rule is to allow a facilitator, or member of the team to request that a "break" be taken from the issue in order to discuss the dynamics existing within the group. It is this process observation and discussion that allow the group to learn from experience. We can assess whether we are using our skills and following agreed-upon structure. Dysfunctional activities that get in the way can also be identified.

Typical questions used in processing may include:

Who are the most active contributors?
Are there team members who are not talking?
What is the emotional atmosphere in the group?
How varied are ideas or viewpoints presented?
Are all viewpoints valued?
Are team members sticking to the subject?
Are there side conversations?
Are people listening to each other?
Are members clarifying the positions of others?
Are people taking ownership for their positions?

Action Activities

Some kinds of team building practice involve the opportunity to physically work together to achieve a goal. Examples of these kinds of group activities include:

- Using specified objects to construct something that is representative of the team
- Completing an obstacle course
- Mastering outdoor challenge experiences
- Playing a team sport

The idea behind activities of this kind is to put us into working relationships that require dependence upon one another while working on things that may be frustrating. These activities allow transfer of experience to real-life pressure situations. There are hundreds of activities of this type that can be done indoors at training sessions or retreats.

There is also a movement aimed at more active involvement by having team members participate in outdoor activities such as mountain climbing, river rafting, backpacking, and the like, where physical participation is a must. Some believe that this approach produces a stronger bond among team members and a higher level of personal satisfaction as the team accomplishes its goals. Whether the outcome from these activities is worth the expense and the resistance sometimes encountered is a question that must be answered in local circumstances.

When properly conceived and processed these activities can be of great value. Because of the potential for intense emotional or physical involvement, the need for proper planning and professional processing is critical. There is abundant learning potential in such activity, but all will be lost without the proper environment and support.

The Total Communication Picture

As team members are taught and given opportunity to practice new skills for seeking and evaluating information, they must also pay close attention to three major dimensions of communication.

Words: First and most obvious are the words that we use. For many, this is the only dimension that is considered when delivering or evaluating communication. If we limit ourselves only to the evaluation of words, we will be missing much of what is really being said. Consider that a person can be using words like "I feel great" in two entirely different ways. In one case, the person may mean "I am feeling wonderful," yet when said in a sarcastic tone, these same words may mean that things couldn't get much worse.

Tone: The second part of the message exists in the tone of voice that accompanies words that are often very carefully chosen. The tone of voice can give clues to the level of energy or commitment that exists, regardless of the words being spoken.

Body Language: A third element is the non-verbal language that is transmitted by the body. Although it can be dangerous to act on an assumption based solely on "body language," these cues can be used as tips that can be "checked out" to confirm or reject a perception. If people seem to be pulling back or looking away it might indicate that what is being said is not having a positive effect. Or, if other members of the team are looking at each other and rolling their eyes, it's best to think about what might be turning them off.

Putting Cues Together: Being able to identify, evaluate, and act upon perceptions gained from these kinds of cues can enable a good team member to function better in every aspect of personal and professional operation.

Think about the ramifications of dealing with a sensitive issue by telephone. Here, the ability to observe non-verbal body messages is not possible. By some estimates, when non-verbal behavior is eliminated, we may be missing more than half of the message. Based on this, it may be a good rule not to deal with sensitive issues over the telephone unless it is unavoidable.

When dealing with something difficult, it's best to have all the cues available in order to better understand what's going on with the people we've got to work with. If you must deal with a crisis via telephone, work particularly hard to focus on the tone of voice being used. Without the non-verbal, you have already lost a big part of the picture. Your best hope is to pick up on whether the tone of voice seems congruent with the words being said. If you notice incongruence, devise a question that can be used to check out your suspicion that what is being said doesn't represent how the person really feels.

The same thing is true for every interaction. Listen to the words, hear the tone, and see the body messages. These signals help us to determine whether we are truly on the same page. The more sensitive the issue, the more important it is that we are able to observe congruency between words, tones, and body messages.

Props and Tools

When training and practicing skills, encourage the use of props and tools that make understanding more effective. These can include the use of charts, overheads, television, video, audio, computers and other creative devices. Familiarity with these tools can insure that everyone in the group is focused on the item a presenter is discussing. The communication process is complex. To assume that one can stand in front of a group and make a point in a casual manner may be a big mistake, especially when talking about a high stakes issue.

14

Time as Context

Technically, measurement of time is related to the earth's rotation around the sun and how the sun fits into larger mechanisms like solar systems and galaxies. Yet, even with a hard science framework, it can still seem that a moment in time is longer or shorter depending on the personal pressure or satisfaction we are experiencing.

Personal Perception

Consider what it was like when you were in elementary school. Was time different when you were on summer vacation? How did time move when you were waiting in anticipation of your fifth birthday party or on the eve of an important holiday? How has time seemed to move during the good and bad times in your life?

Each of us has a personal context for time. It's based on things like age, personality style, belief system, and level of satisfaction with work or personal life. For some, time has a sense of urgency; for others, a sense of calm. Each of us relates to the management of time based on our passion, commitment, habits, attitudes, and the structure within which we operate.

If we have a somewhat mellow personality style, own the business, feel secure about our job, and income projections are up, we may experience little stress about time. On the other hand, if we are insecure, feel little personal satisfaction, have a strong desire to advance, or want to increase production; we may feel more urgency about how time is used.

Those with an outgoing personality style may prefer an unstructured approach to time and issue management. Those with a more control-oriented style may want a very detailed time management approach. And those of us who have had a close look at our own mortality may place a very high value on how our time is spent.

As difficult as it may be, and with all the personal issues involved in how we relate to time, it appears that the better we manage the time that we have available, the higher the probability we will be satisfied and successful. Time is probably the fairest of all resources simply because we all have the same amount and it is our choice as to how we put it to use and to our benefit.

To work effectively with the time we are allotted, it is helpful to plan in segments. Segments can include a lifetime, years, months, weeks, days, hours, or moments. Each of these designations is helpful as we plan and set goals. Even if a goal or dream might take a lifetime to achieve, we must manage the time on a moment-by-moment basis, twenty-four hours per day, seven days per week, as long as our desires remain important. If one desires to be a company president or a good family member, it is through the identification of barriers, useful strategies, and a time line that makes the desire a possibility.

Feelings and Philosophy

As we tackle management of time, one of our biggest obstacles can be handling our feelings. Many times, when it comes to doing the things necessary to make progress, we simply "don't feel like it." Hard as it is, our feelings must be managed. I've heard it said that the difference between a professional and an amateur is that when something needs doing, the amateur will do it as long as it feels good and the professional will do it whether it feels good, or not.

Adding Structure

The management of time is an issue to include in your model. First, it's important to develop an understanding of time and to devise a tangible structure to deal with it. On one level, you deal with time in a philosophical manner by establishing goals and objectives, starting with lifetime desires and working down to management of days, weeks, months, and years.

On a concrete level, you should have a system to help manage time. The system can even become a visual image associated with participation on a particular team. The visual image also creates a perception that planning and use of time is important. A visual symbol can include a loose-leaf notebook or an electronic record-keeping device. Encourage team members to take it everywhere - even to lunch.

Since living a successful life requires keeping track of responsibilities, active use of a time management system helps us to better handle personal and professional obligations. Time is best managed when all facets of job and personal life are integrated in your management system. For people to achieve a sense of satisfaction there must a balance in job and personal life. If your son has a science fair on a Wednesday at 6:00 p.m., that time slot is just as viable for attendance at the science fair as anything else that might come up. That is not to say that your son's science fair project would win the slot every time, but it does create the mind-set that we should evaluate time with regard to all facets of our life and not arbitrarily give away any portion without conscious awareness.

Mutual Needs

If we are conscious about all the things that are important in our lives, we are in a better position to manage our time more effectively. With that awareness, we can examine our activities knowing that there is always a stress between personal or family needs and the needs of organizations or clients. Being conscious of these things and being relentless in using a record keeping system puts a handle on time and keeps us in touch with what we are sacrificing as well as what we are achieving.

At Peace with Time

In conjunction with a time management effort, which applies to your whole life, there are some basic principles that been consistently helpful:

- Keep a clean: house, office, and car
- Get rid of unused, especially clothing and paper
- Fix or discard the broken
- Return the borrowed
- Retrieve the loaned
- Balance the checkbook
- Update finances
- Organize records and files
- Update communications, if only to confirm status
- Know status of all your responsibilities
- When unsure - ask; don't wait
- Be relentless about details and follow-up
- Maintain a tickler file and update others
- Move the ball off your court as quickly as possible
- Maintain the human condition: body and mind

These things sound simple. If they can be mastered and scheduled, greater peace of mind is available. That peace of mind provides a foundation to produce more satisfaction and a greater sense of accomplishment.

Leaders are often acknowledged for what gets done. If we can't complete something, the next best thing is to know its status. Knowing status infers we are on top of things. Management of time and evaluation of what is accomplished can help us escape the trap of working on things that may not make a difference in our personal or professional lives.

How we manage time is a habit or pattern. That habit or pattern includes everything we do. If our pattern is not producing what we want, we can change it. Using a concrete system gives us the vehicle to structure and evaluate change.

One of the most powerful influences of the perception that others have of us is a result of what we do and how well we keep our word. To enhance that part of perception requires that we manage our time, make agreements carefully, tell what we know for sure, explain what is in process and let others know when we will know more.

15

Acknowledgment and Unity

One of our biggest challenges is to find ways to earnestly tell others that they are doing a good job. If this is not done as a conscious effort, it's easy to be caught up in a mind-set that there are so many problems we don't deserve acknowledgment just because we solved one.

If we allow this kind of thinking to dominate, we can find ourselves burned out, and generally discouraged much of the time. We've got to develop a discipline for acknowledging others. We've got to make it a point to look for things that can be legitimately reinforced.

Personal Acknowledgment

One of the best moves you can make is a commitment to acknowledge a specific number of people in a specified time period, preferably in writing, and to keep a record of your success at reaching that goal.

The impact of this kind of effort is very powerful. Generally speaking, people are not accustomed to being acknowledged. When singled out for doing a good job, some don't believe it. Often, it is as if the person is almost embarrassed and not sure how to react, but the acknowledgment always seems to be appreciated. Regular use of acknowledgment reinforces people's understanding that it is the contributions that they make every day that keeps a good organization on track.

To help keep focused on this commitment, write the word "acknowledgment" at the top of every page in your planning calendar. After that word you record a number. That number represents where you are with your commitment. Each day add the number of acknowledgments completed. If none, add zero. Each day carry the total forward.

Notes may be handwritten; typed, or via e-mail. Sometimes, more than one person may get the same note if each worked on the same project. When acknowledging a group, the text should be focused very specifically on what was accomplished. Occasionally, a list-processed letter can be sent to a department or an entire staff.

List processing is the least desirable and most apt to look phony as a method of acknowledgment. It works better when an atmosphere based on individual and small team acknowledgment has been established first. If a large group acknowledgment is interjected in an environment where people do not believe that their efforts are noticed or appreciated, it may be seen as yet another phony attempt to manipulate, rather than as a sincere effort to acknowledge good work or a strong commitment.

It's much easier to select language for an individual hand-written note than it is for a large group acknowledgment. This is because for an acknowledgment to have an impact it must be seen as directly connected to the individual. "You're a wonderful person" and "I'm glad you are on my team" might sound good the first time but after the second or third time team members will begin to wonder exactly what it is that you are trying to do.

Another common misconception about writing acknowledgments is that something astounding must happen in order to justify the effort. This couldn't be further from the truth. There are hundreds of things going on in organizations every day that are special and contribute to overall success.

Group Acknowledgment

When writing a list-processed letter to commend a large group or entire staff, it should be done for excellent or extraordinary work that recipients can identify as having been accomplished through cooperative effort. Sometimes, this effort might be hanging in there through difficult circumstances; other times the focus may be on meeting a group goal, achieving a service rating, or moving into a new facility. Preparation of such an acknowledgment usually involves writing several drafts prior to selection of the final wording. Such a letter should be submitted to trusted individuals for screening of each draft. Their thoughts and suggestions about the impressions that might be elicited by the letter can then be taken into consideration as each new draft is developed.

Send It Home

Mailing an acknowledgment, particularly a group acknowledgment, to an individual's home and starting it out with a personal salutation and ending with a hand signature often help in making the point that even if the letter has been sent to a number of people, the contribution of each one has been sincerely appreciated.

In cases where couples are to receive an acknowledgment as part of a group, care should be taken to insure that they do not receive duplicate letters that are exactly the same. Rather, consider including both names on the same letter. When the same letter is sent to a group, it may also be appropriate to add a personal note as a "P.S." when the signature is affixed. When letters of this type are sent to a person's home where they can be opened in the presence of one's family a more powerful impact is achieved. The more personalized and specific the communication is - the more powerful the impact.

If acknowledgments start out as "Dear Staff" or Dear Team," are written in memo form, and are produced on a copy machine, the desired message may not be hitting home. An environment must be created that fosters the understanding that people are valued for individual contribution as well as for their part in the accomplishment of larger projects.

Written versus Verbal

Whether the commitment is to do two acknowledgments per day or one acknowledgment per week is not the important thing. The important thing is that value is placed on letting people know that what they do is important to where the organization is going. Written acknowledgments have been suggested, especially in the beginning, because verbal acknowledgments are easy to divert.

Fact is, in many places, people are unaccustomed to getting a solid pat on the back. Within this reality, if somebody says: "You're doing a great job with the new outreach program," or "That was a great idea on how to organize the transportation department," the compliment may be viewed as an off-hand comment. When that same acknowledgment is in writing, it's like the person has been grabbed by the lapels, snapped to attention, and told that he or she has done something especially important and that you really appreciate it.

If you feel powerless or unable to find the resources to do anything else, there is no excuse for bypassing this one. This may be the single most powerful thing that an individual can do. If you start it and keep it going, others will follow. You'll be amazed at what can happen. Just make sure that each acknowledgement is genuine.

Directing Focus

If you choose to acknowledge the commitment and accomplishments of others, you'll find that you must pay attention to the positive things that are going on in the organization. Don't worry about who is doing it, just take note, and tell her. If a sales person develops excellent customer relations, tell him. If a secretary solves logistical problems as soon as they appear, tell him, if the program chair of your club schedules excellent presenters, tell her. If your daughter helps out at home let her know. And, don't forget to let your mom and dad know that you appreciate the time they spend on your behalf.

It's also O.K. to tell controlling board members when they do something that you think is commendable. Some of them won't admit it, but it probably thrills them when they get a positive acknowledgment. After all, they're just like everybody else. They work hard, they get criticized for the things that go wrong, and they may never get a compliment for a job well done.

It's even O.K. to tell your boss she did something right. We sometimes seem to have a mentality that suggests that all acknowledgments are supposed to come down from above. For some reason, it doesn't occur to people that those in supervisory positions can also use an occasional "attaboy" or "attagirl." Supervisors are human too. They can get down, depressed, and be low on energy when all they hear about are things that are going wrong.

16

Marketing and Perception

Most organizations deal with extremely diverse value and belief systems that have been programmed by substantially different generational conditions. These differences guarantee that there will be different points of view on virtually every issue. For this reason a continuous marketing and communications program is critical.

When considering a marketing approach, a major pitfall that must be overcome is the belief that we must wait for a big breakthrough to justify talking up what's good in our organization. Actually, marketing need not be centered on creating this type of hype. It can be a focused process designed to identify problems, provide education about options, and acknowledge success.

To magnify the problem of how difficult it can be to keep organizations in a positive light: it's important to understand that society generally tends to focus on the negative. Some estimates suggest that as much as 80 percent of what people talk about and what is reported through media sources is centered on negative outcomes or speculation about negative situations.

If we can accept the possibility that people tend to develop some personal programming based on what they see, feel, and hear the most often, then we should see the danger in allowing people's attention to freely wander.

A good organization never leaves "image" to chance. Consider why large corporations spend so much to develop and present a positive center of attention. The answer has got to be tied to the knowledge that if image were left to chance it could easily end up landing on the negative end of the perception continuum.

Subtle Communication

To further explore how marketing and public relations can affect the way an organization is perceived, think about what happens when you're sitting home, relaxing and watching television. You're enjoying one of your favorite shows and up comes a commercial. The commercial might be for Burger King, Wendy's, McDonald's, or some special restaurant in your home-town. Maybe you don't even pay particular attention to what's going on in the commercial. You turn your attention to other things and only occasionally glance at the pictures while the music and dialogue play in the background.

Then the commercial is over and your favorite show starts again. Everything is going along fine, then all of the sudden, you notice that you are starting to feel hungry. Is that an accident? For many, that hunger is no accident. It is directly related to that short programming bit or an accumulation of them.

The impact of a commercial is enhanced by the number of times a similar message has been heard. No doubt, it also ties into many other life experiences. If we've always enjoyed a good hamburger, a great looking picture of a hamburger might trigger thoughts and desires that lead us to consider going to a favorite restaurant.

If this seems farfetched, consider how many decisions made by people you know were based on programming that was first received through a planned marketing effort and later reinforced in personal conversation. Take, for example, the cars we drive. Many people buy cars based on an image that is created in the media. Once the purchase commitment is made, a person has 'bought' the image. From this point on, in order to support his own self-concept the purchaser reinforces his decision as he talks with others about the very things that sold him on the car in the first place.

Given, occasionally a person makes a purchase, regrets it, and then gets even by being super critical of the product. More often, once convinced to buy, it is very difficult to change positions unless something drastic happens. Once committed, many feel foolish if they can't represent the item positively to friends and acquaintances. Even when people decide that they don't like something, they often work very hard at getting out from under it gracefully. No way do we want others to think that we didn't have our act together when we decided to make the purchase in the first place.

If you can honestly say that you and others you know are not affected in the ways I am suggesting, then you probably don't need a marketing or public relations program. If, on the other hand, you can see some validity in what is suggested, you should consider that the perception people will have about your organization should not be left to chance any more than major automakers would leave the perception of their automobiles to chance.

Successful organizations make every effort to promote both tangible and aesthetic aspects of their products or services. People who operate successful businesses also understand that problems may arise with their products and services and that some word of those negatives will get around. They know that if they don't create a balance that favors their positive side, they could be out of business. A good marketing expert can take a problem requiring recall and turn it into a positive by emphasizing the integrity and service of the company.

Another misconception about developing a marketing plan is that it must be built on some monumental breakthrough. But when was the last time you can remember a truly monumental break-through? Even those things that seem to be big a breakthrough are often based on small steps forward. Really big breakthroughs are hard to come by. Yet for some reason, we are often unwilling to talk about the good things we do unless we think we've just discovered cold fusion.

A Marketing Plan

When putting together a marketing effort, we must start where we are. Look around, there are positive things going on in your organization. Identify them and find ways to talk about them. Form a team of people who have both an interest and some expertise in understanding what other people perceive as positive.

Create opportunities for those people to meet, discuss the situation, and devise strategies to get the word out. This can mean getting together once per month, perhaps over breakfast or lunch. The job is to look at the current situation and into the future. Work to get the word out on things that have already been accomplished, identify actions taken to manage difficult situations, and plan marketing strategies to give advanced notice of difficult situations to be faced. To stimulate thinking on possible issues that could arise, here is a list of topics accumulated through the work of such a committee:

Pubic Relations Project List

- Biweekly staff newsletter
- Staff discussion groups
- Current and former board member recognition
- 20-year staff recognition
- Perception surveys
- Organization newsletter
- Visual electronic presentation
- Community and staff relations committee
- Board of directors programs
- Staff training about public relations
- Programs for community organizations
- Anniversary events
- Volunteer recognition
- Staff updates on finances, & market share.
- Annual "Thank You" list
- Marketing plan
- Media releases
- Annual report

- "Good News" notes
- Board of directors recognition of staff
- Press packets for board meetings
- Community information lunches
- Special topic meetings and presentations
- Relationships with political sub-divisions
- Community discussion forums
- Billboard project
- Graphics work for publication covers
- Certificates
- Newspaper recognition
- Quality management results
- Work with service organizations
- Buildings and grounds improvement
- Recruitment of staff
- Political climate
- Economic stability and growth
- Upcoming trouble spots

When considering how to move forward with internal communication or to external audiences, the marketing team uses the skills and concepts from the team model to do planning, agree on individual responsibilities and provide for accountability. Marketing in this way develops confidence in what's been done and helps people prepare for actions needed in the future.

Planning Sequence for Marketing

The following is a general approach that can be useful when planning a marketing and communications program. This process is also an example of how the basic problem-solving model, presented earlier, can be adaptable to any setting.

A. Identify Problem(s)

- Brainstorm or list accumulated issues. Use consensus or straw vote to determine a priority order for problems identified. Select and clearly define the tasks that will be immediately undertaken. Place remaining problems on a list, in a file, for continued review along with new issues.

B. Establish Criteria for Success

- Identify what must be achieved in the short and long-term.

C. Identify Elements Impacting the Issue

What groups are impacted?
- Are there trends to be considered?
- What data exists regarding the issue?
- What opinion exists surrounding the issue?
- What assumptions exist related to the issue?
- What values exist as "filters" in the group(s) or audience(s) to be communicated with?
- What new information do we need?

D. Direction

- What will we communicate?
- Who will get the information?
- Do we have vehicles to communicate with impacted groups?
- What new vehicles are needed to fill the gaps?

E. Implementation

- How to communicate with impacted groups?
- Who will do the communicating?

- Exactly what will be communicated?
- Who will receive the communication?
- When will the communication take place?
- How will in-process effectiveness be evaluated?
- How will "mid-stream" changes be made?

F. Follow-up

- Who will follow-up each element?
- How do we test our assumptions about what will work (i.e. surveys, etc.)?
- How will project success be evaluated?
- When will we assess success and determine if change is needed?

Where to Focus

As a marketing team works, it is important to recognize both internal and external audiences. Many times, much emphasis is placed on external constituents. Meanwhile, those on staff remain in the dark. Nothing hurts credibility more than a marketing program that sends information outward while staff is bewildered about what is going on.

Marketing as Manipulation

Another marketing misconception is centered on the question: "Is marketing a way of manipulating people into believing that there are good things happening?" The answer here is clear. The secret to a good marketing program comes from dealing truthfully with circumstances that exist. That means making sure that the good things that happen are reinforced. It also requires knowing what stakeholders are thinking about, what their solid opinions are, and where they are confused.

It is only with this kind of understanding that we can educate others about the realities faced and progress being achieved. Without this context many people will choose to live in a fantasy world that includes expectations that are impossible to meet. If we allow ourselves to be set up in this fashion, we can only lose.

Spotlight Talent

In service organizations, a significant facet of a larger marketing program should include provision for all team members to have access to the spotlight in a way that validates professional competence and commitment.

In any organization, particularly those that involve hundreds or thousands of people, it is inevitable that questions will arise and hard feelings will exist. This reality is made worse because people tend to focus more on negative information and rumors of negative situations than they do on positive aspects. Because of this, it is extremely important to get team members up front at board meetings, with clients, at community groups, and in every possible media source where their expertise can be spotlighted and validated.

This begins to create a positive context so that when a negative situation occurs, it can be considered along with the positives that have also been seen and heard.

Celebrate Victories

Just as some organizations find little time to market their successes, they frequently ignore their victories. If you are going to maintain the energy to continue to fight the never-ending battle to survive and grow, you've got to use the energy that can be gleaned from recognizing and celebrating victories.

One of the best examples of this rule was observed in a program designed to deal with clients having severe emotional disorders. This program was renowned for its creativity and innovation. The staff was highly trained, the facilities were excellent, and needed resources were available. In spite of all these positives the burnout rate for personnel was a puzzle to all.

As the situation was analyzed, it became clear that the most significant factor related to burnout was the inability to see progress. Once this was identified, a system was developed that more clearly tracked behavioral changes. This information was then formatted in such a way that the staff could tell when they were making progress. Once progress could be seen and victories could be celebrated, the situation with staff burnout improved. There was less turnover, and more job satisfaction. This shows how energy to go forward can come from victories, which if not observed, may totally escape our awareness.

When a team goes against an opponent that is bigger and has been established longer, a good showing can be reason to celebrate. You don't need to wait until you've reached your final goal. Set benchmarks, even small ones. Their accomplishment can serve as inspiration to make the next jump.

17

Focus Groups and Forums

If you have hierarchical power over others, getting them to see you as a person, not just a position is a significant challenge. If you don't work in close proximity to teammates, your challenge is especially difficult. The question is, does the "real you" get through?

Size Makes a Difference

Two-way communication is vital to the development of a sense of team and it's a lot easier to talk about than to realize. In smaller systems, the process is less complicated. Your office may be in the same building where most of the staff works. You may have automatic daily contact. You see them in the workroom, at lunch, and in the hallways. You may even attend some of the same community functions. Two-way communication is so much a matter of course that you never think of it as a "process" requiring special attention. In this situation the probability of staff members knowing the real you, your positions on issues, and your ideals, is pretty good.

In larger organizations, seeing and talking with staff members isn't automatic. Size inhibits communication. When offices are in different buildings and team members are spread over miles, physical distance can easily translate into personal distance. In such a situation, leaving communication to chance is risky business. People you don't see regularly may base their perceptions not on who you are, but as other people portray you.

This presents two choices. You can count on others to represent you accurately, or you can devise ways to meet directly with those you don't ordinarily see. A combination of these approaches is best of all.

Staff Discussion Groups

One excellent approach to increase contact is through structured discussion groups composed of six to twenty staff members. The purpose of such groups is to hear concerns, answer questions, and generally keep in touch with current thinking.

The decision to use discussion groups should not be made lightly. Depending on past history, some people may wonder about the motives behind the group. In some cases staff could reject the idea and as a result, group discussion would be reserved, stilted, and viewed as an attempt to manipulate. Fortunately, if properly founded and with care given to the process, most of these concerns can be alleviated. Even if some tension is evident during the first sessions, it can quickly dissipate and subsequent discussions will be open, candid, and valuable.

Selecting Participants

A good approach is to start by holding groups organized so that work friends and acquaintances come at the same time. You also need to decide which members of the management staff should attend each group discussion. Its good if the CEO or division head can attend the meetings. This indicates that the gatherings are important. Other managers or supervisors should be selected to insure that there are experts present who can answer questions and discuss issues from all perspectives.

To select participants, gather employee rosters from each department. Then apportion the number of total slots available so that larger departments or job classifications have the largest number of participants.

Do not play favorites. Randomly select a name on each roster to serve as a starting point. Then count by sevens to arrive at the names of participants to fill available slots. In each subsequent session, continue the random selection process, passing over personnel that have already attended a group. Make it known how the participants are chosen to scotch the idea that you are setting up an elite support group.

Personal Invitation

Once participants are identified, send a personal note inviting each of them to join the discussion group. In the letter, state the ground rules for the group, and let people know that all supervisors have been informed about who is being invited. The word "invitation" is emphasized because this is no command performance. Staff members who find it inconvenient to attend should RSVP so that others can be invited. Their names can then be put back on the roster for possible invitation at a later time.

Participants can be changed at every meeting. This gives a broad exchange of ideas. No one should be invited to attend the discussion group a second time until everyone in a department or job classification has the opportunity to attend a group session.

Scheduling Sessions

A good structure is to hold a discussion session each month, during the workday, in a room that is large enough to hold the group comfortably but small enough to encourage informality. Arrange chairs in a circle or horseshoe so participants can talk face to face and there are no barriers to inhibit discussion.

Discussion Format

As participants arrive, offer them refreshments. Use this informal time to make contact with individual participants. Next, review the purpose of the meeting and the ground rules you would like to follow. state that the goal is to get to know one another better and discuss issues of interest to them. Make it clear that there is no predetermined agenda.

Schedule a session for two hours and divide it into two parts: First, the participants introduce themselves and tell the group something about their job assignments and prior experiences either in the organization or in general. During that part of the process, take every opportunity to acknowledge participants for the things that they are doing to contribute to the success of the organization.

End the session when discussion is closed. Don't prolong to fill the two hours if the energy isn't there. Once trust is established, it is more likely that you will run over your time than end early.

Be sure to encouraged participants to "say a little more" about their work. Many times, committed and hard-working people tend to downplay their contributions. One goal is to draw them out to increase their peers' awareness and so that they can be acknowledged. Also encourage participants to talk about any personal experiences or interests they would like to mention. Group leaders can model this by telling about things that are going on in their family, or with their hobbies.

Next, take a break for a snack. During the break, ask participants to list the issues they want to talk about during the second part of the session. You can ask participants to write these items anonymously on small slips of paper. Then collect and compile them into a rough agenda and post it on a chart.

As time passes, participants may not want or need this anonymous status. When that happens, just ask group members to jot down their items on a piece of hanging chart paper during the coffee break.

It is from this participant-initiated agenda that discussion emerges on just about every imaginable topic. You may encounter interest in everything from computer software to parking lot security or the septic system. To give you an idea of how vast the potential, here is a partial list of topics that have emerged in this type of group:

- Computer training
- Safe drinking water
- Career counseling
- Staff development
- Building temperatures

- Rumor control
- Parking lot security
- Snow removal
- Equipment and furniture
- Staff cutbacks
- Gas pump accessibility
- Potholes in driveways
- Marketing
- Carpet vs. tile floors
- Maintaining standards
- Broken windows and doors
- Inspections
- Ethnic and racial concerns
- Computer software
- Smoking
- Hiring supervisors
- Board- staff relations
- Arrival and departure
- Professional meeting funds
- Phone calls
- Early retirement
- Purchasing
- Salting slippery sidewalks
- Legislation
- Professional standards
- Case or work loads
- Policy and procedures
- Status of competitors
- Market share

This list portrays the broad potential that exists for discussion material. To help encourage discussion, you can post the charts from previous sessions so new groups can be reminded about how wide-ranging the discussion can be.

In the letter of invitation, tell those invited to check with others in their department to see if they have suggestions about topics that should be discussed. You will find that representatives from some departments come to the group discussion with their own list. Others may come with suggestions from close friends. In other settings, it may become routine to post a sheet in a workroom or other gathering place so topics can be listed to be taken to the group for discussion.

It's amazing how often discussion of an issue will clear up something that is bothering an individual or group. It's also interesting how often information surfaces that can be used in future planning and problem solving. One of the things that is important in maintaining the integrity of this type of group process is to never guaranteed results you cannot produce.

Follow-up

After every session, send notes to each participant acknowledging individual contribution and, when appropriate, inviting further involvement. You may want to put a summary of the discussion topics and a list of participants in your regular staff newsletter. From that point on, you can rely on the grapevine to spread information. Invite those who want to know more about an issue to talk to a member of the particular group that was involved in its discussion.

There is some risk that positions can be slanted when relayed to others not in attendance. It is also likely that information reported from colleagues will have high integrity. These are the factors that you must balance when you decide how to report the information generated in your group. You can also bet that if something is not cleared up, it will come up again in a later group.

On a periodic basis, you may decide to print a status report on items that have been resolved as a result of their identification during the discussions. The goal here is to convey to the staff that even though all problems can't be solved right away, you are making an effort to deal with the things that they bring forward.

Tips on Process

For this kind of discussion group to work, there are a few cautions to bear in mind. First, it takes someone with facilitation skill to help keep the discussion on track. Facilitation skills are an adaptation of the skills outlined earlier as basic skills. Also, it's important to have on hand those with technical and logistical information to answer questions that might come up based on the makeup of the group.

Second, don't be surprised if conversation doesn't flow easily at first. The personalities of the participants, what's going on in the organization, the past history of staff communication - all these factors have an impact. Once staff members realize that you have nothing up your sleeve, these kinds of problems should disappear.

Third, don't worry that you won't have anything to talk about. Even without a predetermined agenda, it's unlikely that you'll have a shortage of topics to discuss.

Finally, be honest and open. Enter each group discussion with the intention of being open to any topic, even ones that make you uncomfortable. Be prepared to respond to each concern with a direct answer, an explanation of why a direct answer isn't available, or with a commitment to follow through and provide an answer at a later date.

Positive Fallout

You'll be amazed about the number of problems identified that otherwise would fall through the cracks, and once brought into focus are easily solved. Just the small gesture of paying more attention to getting salt onto the sidewalks can show that you are interested in making things better.

As time passes, the nature of discussion groups can be modified to fit changing circumstances. You can hold groups to deal with specific topics of importance. These sessions give staff members a chance to exchange views and perspectives, air concerns, and learn the why and how of all facets of operation. It also gives everyone an opportunity to get to know his or her colleagues better.

Outreach Forums

In addition to surveys and interviews, it seems natural that another way to convey a desire for an open system is to model that behavior by participating in discussions with groups made up of representatives of audiences served. Again, the goal is to find out what people are thinking and to clarify what you are about.

Inviting Participants

One way to select participants for outreach groups is to give key members of your staff the responsibility to identify people and write a personal letter inviting them to a forum. In the invitation, tell people that you want to know what they think about your operation - both good and bad. The discussion agenda may focus on the topics they suggest as well as specific issues you identify. You can also invite them to bring friends or colleagues if they so desired. The option to bring along a companion or associate serves both to increase attendance and make people more comfortable.

Impact of the Invitation

The purpose of the invitation is to encourage people to attend the group. Often, if there is just a general notice that a forum will be held, people may perceive that it is intended for someone else. By using an invitation, you can do a better job of recruiting a base of participants that can provide you with information you need. This does not preclude allowing open attendance.

Unless there is a mandatory nature to the invitation, attendance can be short of 100% of those invited. At first cut, this may seem disappointing. In reality, the positives gained are not just a result of those who attend the forum. Each person who receives an invitation is impacted. Even people who do not attend may thank you for the invitation and for being interested in their ideas and opinions.

Organization and Logistics

At an outreach forum, you can follow the same basic process used with staff groups. Use the first part of the session for informal conversation (of course, while enjoying refreshments), then move on to build the agenda and discuss the issues.

Although you will occasionally feel like you have been "roughed up" in these groups, the end result is that you will be better able to plan and problem-solve because you have a clear picture of the value structure of those you serve and, in some cases, of barriers to be overcome.

18

Facilitation and Consensus

Consider the following scenario: As CEO, your conservative approach to managing finances has always kept the budget in the black. Even so, financial projections indicate the organization cannot continue operating beyond the current year without additional resources.

Opinions vary widely. Some are advising to run in the red and bet on future revenue for a bail out. A leading businessman who heads your board of directors says this approach would be irresponsible. He lobbies for severe cuts, including pay. Rumblings from the union suggest staff will walk out if they don't get the salary increases and load reductions they're demanding.

Win, Lose, or Draw

What do you do? The wrong choice - or a good choice made at the wrong time - could leave you standing alone. At first, choices seem clear-cut: either burrow in and wait for events to take their own course, or take charge and dictate a course of action. A third, option is to act as facilitator: bring people face-to-face with all the facts and feelings involved, and work for a consensual solution that can be supported under fire.

A Matter of Opinion

The facilitator recognizes that when no obvious answer appears, it's best to build on the brainpower of everyone involved. The facilitator listens to all viewpoints, analyzes the problem from every perspective, and uses multiple perspectives to resolve an issue. Simply put, a facilitator realizes other people have brains, too. Believing this truth - and following a few basic guidelines - a facilitator can begin developing support toward a reasonable solution.

Facilitation can be effective in any group situation and it is an excellent tool for use with boards of directors staff and clients. This overview discusses facilitation with board members and others, in several scenarios. The basic tenets included are applicable to any group.

Judging Decisions

For a decision to be considered "good," it must be acceptable to those who will be impacted. It's also important to remember that what a group in one organization considers appropriate might not work elsewhere. The right decision is the one that makes sense where you are.

If the organization is headed into the red ink, you might choose to increase costs, run into a deficit, borrow money, shut down, deny raises, reorganize services or change product production. On face value, any one of these options might be considered the answer in someone's point of view. A facilitator works for the decision that is acceptable in the specific situation. The facilitation process draws on everyone involved to identify a multitude of options, and settle on a workable solution.

Why It Works

A leader who acts as facilitator has the advantage of using the power inherent in a formal position along with informal power to make things work. Informal power comes from a collaboration that allows people to explore problems together in unconventional ways. This collaborative, participatory approach creates shared responsibility, and it works at all points in an organization.

A good secretary or administrative assistant exemplifies this approach. They're often on the front line acting as a skilled facilitator by taking a neutral stance at the beginning of a conflict. He listens carefully, is nonjudgmental, routes the problem to the appropriate individual or office, then follows up to ensure that the problem does not get lost in the shuffle.

As a facilitator, it's important to make room for any viewpoint or position, especially in the early stages of discussion. By not becoming defensive about opinions you don't agree with, an open atmosphere helps create options that ultimately bring people together.

This openness might not come easily. Most people tend to go into a situation with a pre-established position or bias, even if they are not conscious about it. The trick is to recognize that we all have this tendency.

To help people express their predetermined ideas, listen carefully, and repeat what you hear in your own words. After all positions are clearly established, you can help the group look for points in common and then get the facts and opinions needed to mediate differences.

It takes skill to get issues and opinions out in a nonjudgmental way, but this open and accepting approach to decision making helps establish the trust needed to resolve differences.

Many alternatives are available to help discover a wide range of opinions: discussion groups, public hearings, surveys, individual discussions, committee study, work sessions, and formal public meetings, to name just a few. In all of these kinds of activities, the aim is to clarify problems and be open to all viewpoints. As a result, when the time comes to make a decision, those involved have a better understanding of both the facts and emotions surrounding the issue.

No Panacea

The facilitator approach might not work in all situations. If others place political ambition above the general good, or are more interested in advancing their careers than in working together, you have to watch your back and be prepared for frustration. When it works well, though, the facilitator approach ensures a high level of involvement and increases the likelihood that everyone will support a decision, even a difficult or uncomfortable one.

19

Stress and Self-Preservation

Management of stress is an asset to performance as well as to personal preservation. Sources of stress can be obvious or unsuspected.

To put the complex issue of stress into context, it's crucial to recognize that any system, from a family to a large organization is capable of draining all of a person's energy. This point has been stated very carefully, and it is not intended to insinuate that individuals from your family, organization, or staff would intentionally want to cause harm. The system as a whole, however, can be impersonal and does not necessarily operate in the caring manner that another human might show. Because of this, it's important to carefully assess what it takes to insure our personal well-being and to insert support systems into our lives where possible.

What Works for You

The reason it is so difficult to manage stress is that what works as a stress reliever for one person may be a stress inducer for another.

If you and some of your friends were asked to make a list of things that you believe would relieve stress, it's likely that the list would contain many of these items.

- Deep breathing
- Reading
- Time alone
- Laughter

- Vacation
- A day off
- Exercise
- Shopping

- Music
- Fishing
- Hobbies
- Divorce
- Marriage
- Talking
- Napping

- Meditation
- Prayer
- Drugs and alcohol
- Eating
- Dieting
- Being with people

If you think carefully about this list, you can see that almost any item might cause distress or be a stress reliever, depending on the person and the situation.

As an example, one of the most popular stress release activities is "shopping." For many people, going shopping, indulging themselves, buying something they want, can seem to ease a stressful feeling. The problem is that if we spend more than our budget can support, we may actually induce greater stress when the bills come due. Many people have purchased clothes, cars, boats, and other diversions because they believed that they owed it to themselves because of the work pressure that they had to endure. Only later do they feel the pressure as additional payments increase their level of stress.

Finding the Formula

Managing destructive stress and creating overall wellness is tricky because each one of us has a different way of internalizing our circumstances and each one of us faces a unique set of personal and professional life experiences. One way to simplify the issue is to think about it as related to the "Poker Chip Theory." Following this idea, there are a number of areas in life that may contribute to one's overall well being. Each of these may be considered a chip. The goal is to keep as many of these chips in our pile as possible. If one of the chips slips away or gets out of balance temporarily, we may be able to deal with it because of the rest of the chips in our pile. If we lose to many chips at the same time, our overall level of wellness could be at risk.

It's also important to recognize that individuals may have their own way of defining and maintaining personal well-being. The important point here is for each of us to stay very conscious of what's happening. The imminent danger in not being aware of our personal circumstance was focused by John Fronk as he discussed what might be thought of as "the frog theory." To illustrate, if you were to drop a frog into a pot of boiling water, it would instantly know that it was in a dangerous situation and leap out. But, place that same frog in a pot of tepid water, over a slow flame, and it might very well adapt to the temperature of the slowly heating water until it is eventually overcome. In parallel, a dangerous part of destructive stress may be that we can adjust to it so well that we may not recognize its destructive force until it's too late.

Maintaining a Balance

To make a contribution, you've got to take care of yourself so that you can be around for the long haul. To accomplish this, beware of those who would suggest that you mask symptoms of things that are distressful to you. Our current culture seems to rely heavily on the use of over-the-counter and prescription drugs to make pressure and discomfort disappear. Don't misunderstand; there is nothing wrong with using an appropriate prescription under the guidance of a professional. That is, while you are also dealing with the causes of the symptom. Without dealing with the causes, all that may be accomplished is temporary comfort at the risk of overall well being. As food for thought, here are a few ideas that may be helpful in managing this complex issue.

Balance Comfort and Stress Zone

Be aware of how much time you spend working under stress. Make a conscious effort to balance stressful time with comfortable healing time that helps you to regenerate. Establish supportive activities and do them regularly, be it fishing, reading, going to dinner with the family, visiting relatives, playing cards, or exercising. Find activities that support your sense of well being and make them a habit.

Recognize Strength and Vulnerability

Be aware of how much time you are spending in situations where your style, training, and experience allow you to operate from strength. Recognize the amount of time you spend in situations where these elements make you vulnerable. If you spend a lot of time in vulnerable situations, you should be looking for others who can provide support, and you will likely need more regeneration time.

Don't Fight Losing Battles

Assess, very carefully, how and where you use your energy. Be sure that the achievable outcome is worth the personal price that you will pay for its attainment.

Do Some Regular Physical Activity

Ride a bike, go for a walk, play Ping-Pong, play golf. The options are endless. The important thing is that you find some physical activity that supports your well being. It doesn't have to be high-impact aerobics, running marathons, or pumping iron (although all of those are legitimate options). Make a responsible assessment of what activity will maintain or improve your health as well as your sense of well being. Confer with a physician or other trained professional to determine what best fits your current life situation.

Work on Your Problems

Look closely at the problems you deal with every day. How many of them are yours and how many of them are really the responsibility of someone else? Given the number of problems that a large organization can generate, be sure to apply your energy to the right ones.

Protecting Your Priorities

It is important to manage the time in your life. Be sure that your calendar has time blocked for the activities that contribute to your renewal and to your personal relationships. If you do this, you will be better able to handle your professional responsibilities. If your daughter has a softball game or your son is in a play put it on your appointment calendar. If someone asks you to go to a meeting at that time, tell him or her you have a conflict. Most of the time, people will work with you to find another time of mutual convenience. If you can't find any other time, you may need to change your calendar. But don't assume so at first cut. You don't need to explain every aspect of your life. Your attendance at a family or wellness activity can be just as important, maybe more important, than some professional commitments.

Get Away

Force yourself to take a vacation. You won't believe what a great feeling it is (even if you fret for a few days before you can relax). When you return, not only will you have more energy, you will have a fresh perspective to tackle your problems.

You don't have to go far away. You do have to get disconnected enough to change channels. The length of time varies from person to person. For some, it takes three days to wind down before relaxation can set in. For others, the enjoyment may begin as soon as the grill is lighted, the car is on the road, or the plane is in the air.

Use Positive Self-Talk

There is more and more informed opinion that supports the idea that how we talk to ourselves has an impact on how we feel and how we operate. Be alert to the messages you're sending yourself. If you find yourself dwelling on negative thoughts, you have the power to change that. Consciously develop positive self-talk messages and intentionally use them for personal support.

Capitalizing on Support

We all need support of one kind or another at some time. Think about whom it is that challenges you, makes you laugh, respects confidentiality, and gives you tactful feedback. Seek out the people who make a positive difference in your life. Make it a point to spend time with them. It may be as simple as making contact with a supporter during your coffee break or at lunchtime. Other times, it might require seeking professional help. Remember, to continue to make a contribution to others, taking care of you must also be a priority.

Appendix
Changepoint Perception Assessment

Nature of Perception

When administering this instrument, remember that results are based perception. This means that misunderstanding can be reflected in responses. It can also mean that some responses are based on lack-of or incomplete information. In some cases, information alone may clear up some of the concerns that show up in survey results. In other cases, new information, training, or procedures may be helpful. Most importantly, remember, one's perception is one's current reality.

Focus of Planning

Items that plot highest should be considered for highest priority when devising an improvement plan.

Consider History

It is wise to consider that, if respondents are concerned that they may be evaluated based on how they respond to the instrument, results can show lower need than actually exists. Results may also show lower than expected in a culture which has a very traditional history and which might be thought of (by some) as being 'closed' to ideas involving participation, or joint planning and problem solving

Experience and Intuition

In cases where it is suspected that respondents may feel less than comfortable in providing full disclosure, planning should proceed with a focus on the category items that show highest need, even if they are not in a high or severe problem area.

Distribution of Responses

Response scores may be averaged for each item or for a

category. It may also be useful to consider the distribution of responses. When responses are clustered, it may be that perceptions are similar among respondents. If responses are varied, people have been treated differently, or for some reason may perceive the same actions differently.

Use of Statistical Analysis

Results may be analyzed by various statistical treatments, including: Mean, Range, Standard Deviation, Response Frequency, and Analysis of Variance. Categories or items may be placed on graphs for consideration. Use of means or averages may give a summary picture. Calculation of standard deviation may indicate whether a group opinion is diverse or similar. Frequency of response on an item by item basis may yield more specific data on how to plan for information dissemination, training, or organizational change.

When used with a group or team, you are providing perceptions of how the individuals who make up that team perform, as a composite, on each question in the survey.

When used to assess an individual, this instrument may be used by having a group provide perceptions of a specific individual, then average their responses. These responses may be used independently or compared to a form completed by the same individual on his/her self.

Over all, whether assessing an individual, team, group, or organization the goal is to determine if there is a problem with regard to each item on the survey. Ideally, the response "No Problem" would be the most desirable for each item. Any other response indicates some level of problem. The question then becomes: how big is the problem?

Once the form is completed, either on an organization, team, group, or individual, if it is determined that problems exist, decisions can be made about how much energy should be allocated to its resolution. Perceptions on this survey will help determine both the level of the problem, and the amount of priority that should be placed on improvement.

Results may be used to determine new information needed, training that may be appropriate, or changes that should be considered. The instrument may be completed again after interventions have been made and appropriate time has passed to allow new information, training, or changes to be integrated. A comparison of results from the first and second administration may be used as one measure to gage progress.

To begin the resolution process: Focus groups, teams or individuals who represent survey respondents may be helpful in further breaking down the elements of each problem area. For example: if, in the section on Diversity, item #3, "Understands the concept of age discrimination and operates appropriately in all activity" shows as a priority problem, the individual or group may be asked "what is or could be happening that would create this perception?" The results of the discussion may then be used with other information and ideas available in making a plan to deal with the issue.

Planning: The planning & problem solving process requires expanded information from internal sources as well as from research and informed external sources. It is suggested that a step by step problem solving or planning process be used. It is also suggested that status assessment steps be built into the process.

Lowering Resistance: Individuals, teams, and organizations may resist recognition of a problem. Reducing this resistance requires conscious effort. <u>Continued referral to the concept of perception may be helpful. The concept of perception includes the idea that perception may not be truth as one person or group sees it or intends it but it is the reality for the perceiver.</u> The ultimate goal is to resolve perception problems by taking whatever action may be necessary.

Ultimately: The goal is to create a mind-set that continued assessment will lead to better working conditions as well as increased organizational success.

Changepoint Perception Assessment

Responses on this form will help to evaluate an individual, group, or organization with regard to skills and concepts important to success.

For an individual or group, responses may be considered independently or compared to a self assessment or assessment by others. As you assess an individual or group, determine if there is a problem with regard to each survey item. Ideally, the response "No Problem" is most desirable. Any other response indicates that some problem exists.

To begin, write the name of the individual, or designate the group or organization that will be the focus as you respond to items on the form. Mark only one response for each survey item.

Focus Area: (Person, Group, or Organization)

_____   Date: _____

Degree of Problem Action Needed

None	Slight	Moderate	High	Severe
1	2	3	4	5

The 'Degree of Problem and Action' Scale goes from 1 to 5.

1 = No Problem - No action needed
2 = Slight Problem - Increase understanding
3 = Moderate Problem - Action is needed
4 = Big Problem - Action should be in process
5 = Severe Problem - Action is overdue

Category: People Orientation	1	2	3	4	5
Enhances effectiveness & relationships through use of personality & leadership style	O	O	O	O	O
Lets others know that their values & needs are important and will be considered	O	O	O	O	O
Understands the importance of our history and culture	O	O	O	O	O
Knows the importance of giving and keeping one's word	O	O	O	O	O
Allows people the freedom to operate within clearly defined areas of responsibility	O	O	O	O	O
Maintains a supportive, effective team performance level	O	O	O	O	O

Category: Environment	1	2	3	4	5
Tracks factors outside the organization which can impact success potential	O	O	O	O	O
Insures that what the organization does fits with expectations of owners and clients	O	O	O	O	O

Lets others know that their contributions are valued and foster organization's success	O	O	O	O	O
Creates an atmosphere that allows people to share ideas on any concern or issue	O	O	O	O	O
Establishes and modifies the physical environment to create a good place to work	O	O	O	O	O
Eliminates use of intimidation, harassment, threats, or retaliation	O	O	O	O	O

Category: Communications	**1**	**2**	**3**	**4**	**5**
Uses good listening, paraphrasing, and summarizing skills	O	O	O	O	O
Understands, and responds to the non-verbal communication of others	O	O	O	O	O
Uses appropriate voice-tone, body language and wording when communicating	O	O	O	O	O
Confirms views or positions of others before reaching conclusions	O	O	O	O	O
Uses facilitation skills that support productive group interaction	O	O	O	O	O

	1	2	3	4	5
Uses props and technology to enhance communications	O	O	O	O	O
Uses forums, surveys & other venues to get input from internal audiences	O	O	O	O	O
Uses forums, surveys & other venues to get input from external audiences	O	O	O	O	O
Has a communication structure that provides information inside the organization	O	O	O	O	O
Has a structure to provide information to those outside of the organization	O	O	O	O	O

Category: Diversity

	1	2	3	4	5
Is aware of race and ethnic issues and is sensitive to them in all activity	O	O	O	O	O
Understands concepts of sexual discrimination and harassment and operates appropriately	O	O	O	O	O
Understands the concept of age discrimination and operates appropriately in all activity	O	O	O	O	O

Category: Conflict Resolution	1	2	3	4	5
Understands the nature of conflict and responds to conflict appropriately	O	O	O	O	O
Has procedures for early identification of problems and issues that need attention	O	O	O	O	O
Instills in others a belief that agreements will be kept and that trust is warranted	O	O	O	O	O
Fosters camaraderie with regard to staff and organizational relations	O	O	O	O	O
Creates opportunity for growth and positive change as a result of conflict situations	O	O	O	O	O

Category: Problem Solving	1	2	3	4	5
Uses a clear method for assigning planning & problem solving responsibility	O	O	O	O	O
Uses appropriate questioning techniques to expand understanding & increase options	O	O	O	O	O
Uses comprehensive data and research when problem solving and planning	O	O	O	O	O

	1	2	3	4	5
Uses appropriate processes to resolve value, belief, or opinion based problems	O	O	O	O	O
Uses a process that fosters new and creative, ideas when planning and problem solving	O	O	O	O	O
Uses a participatory, consensus seeking approach when planning and problem solving	O	O	O	O	O
Uses influence effectively, and when needed, uses authority or power appropriately	O	O	O	O	O
Understands the need for verbal and written agreements as a basis for operations	O	O	O	O	O

Categories: Operations	1	2	3	4	5
Has current vision & mission as well as goals which support their attainment	O	O	O	O	O
Develops policies and procedures then clearly communicates them to the people they impact	O	O	O	O	O
Uses a process to encourage improvement of quality and has a structure to gage progress	O	O	O	O	O

Has a staff training and professional growth process that ties to organizational objectives	O	O	O	O	O
Uses strategies for planning and allocation of finances to achieve maximum benefit	O	O	O	O	O
Uses time wisely to organize, resolve issues, solve problems, and accomplish goals	O	O	O	O	O
Uses a staff selection process that furthers the vision and mission of the organization	O	O	O	O	O
Has an appraisal process that helps people meet objectives and prepare for the future	O	O	O	O	O
Holds effective meetings and information sharing sessions as necessary	O	O	O	O	O
Uses a well organized information storage system that is available to those who need it	O	O	O	O	O
Uses a system that appropriately matches work-load with organization objectives	O	O	O	O	O
Represents self and organization in a professional demeanor: manner, character, deportment	O	O	O	O	O

Displays dress and grooming practices that reflect professionally on self and the organization	O	O	O	O	O
Has a clear, understandable system to project future needs	O	O	O	O	O

References & Resources

Changepoint Consulting Service. Offers assistance to individuals and organizations interested in implementing ideas and practices such as those discussed in this book. For additional information: **www.changepoint.org**

Akenhead, James E. **A School Leaders Playbook**. Author House, Bloomington Indiana, 2004.

Edwards, Gerald **Reaching Out**. Innovative Designs for Educational Action, Garden City, NY, 1972.

Fronk, Ron L. **Creating A Lifestyle You Can Live With**. Whitaker House, Springdale PA, 1988.

Gordon, Thomas. **Leader Effectiveness Training**. Putnam, New York, 2001.

Gordon Training International, Thomas Gordon, Ph.D. and Associates. 531 Stevens Avenue West, Solana Beach, CA 92075-2093. Designers of Training Programs including: *Leadership Effectiveness Training, Conflict Resolution, Teacher Effectiveness Training, Parent Effectiveness Training,* and *Mediation Training.* (The author is trained and licensed to present these programs)

Helmstetter, Shad. **What to Say When You Talk to Yourself**. Pocket Books, New York, 1986. (A model for analyzing self-talk and its effect).

Hoy, W., & Miskel, C. **Educational Administration: Theory, Research and Practice**. Random House, New York, 1978. (Regarding Interest and Expertise)

Inscape Publishing Company. Publishers of a variety of instrumentation and workshop formats. 6465 Wayzata Blvd., Suite 800 Minneapolis, MN 55426-1725.
(Inscape sells via licensed consultants. Materials, including the *Personal Profile*, can be ordered from the author).

Prigmore, C., & Atherton, C. **Social Welfare Policy: Analysis and Formulation.** Lexington, Massachusetts: D. C. Heath & Company, 1979 (Regarding criterion for evaluation of decisions and policy)

Massey, Morris. **The People Puzzle.** Reston Publishing Company Inc., Reston VA, 1979. (A variety of video tapes are also available from this author).

Monroe Institute for the Study of Human Consciousness. Lovingston, Virginia, 22949, An organization at the forefront of research and education in exploration of consciousness and in the practical application of its discoveries. (Definitely out-of-the-box thinkers.)

Rowin, Roy. **The Intuitive Manager**. Little, Brown, and Company, Boston and Toronto 1986.

Russell, Ron **Focusing the Whole Brain**. Hampton Roads, Charlottesville Virginia, 2004

Unless You're a Hermit Success Means Working with People

About the Author

Dr. James Akenhead has spent more than four decades helping organizations. This involvement includes: hospitals, banks, local government, pubic schools, universities, counseling agencies, nursing homes, law enforcement, unions, retail sales as well as non-profit service and social organizations. In addition to service as a consultant, he has served as a board member, administrator and officer in a variety of organizations.

Jim has five earned degrees. He has written on leadership and team building in various magazines and journals and has presented at national conferences.

At twenty-six, he was offered his first school superintendent position. His career includes 23 years in local, county, and city superintendence's as well as 20 years as a consultant to public and private sector organizations and as a graduate school instructor.

Jim was selected as a **"Distinguished Graduate of the School of Technology"** at Bowling Green State University and, with his wife Charlene, was chosen as **"Business and Professional Person of the Year"** in their local community. He has been included in seven "who's who" anthologies and The Eye on Education Digest of Innovators. Dr. Akenhead is also the author of A School Leaders Playbook (2004), Uncommon Leadership (2005), School Boards: It's Time To Step Up (2008) and has a chapter titled "Looking at the Frontier" in Focusing the Whole Brain (2004), Edited by Ron Russell.

Jim lives in Alliance, Ohio with his wife Dr. Charlene Akenhead. He notes one of his most interesting experiences, was to backpack the Chilkoot Gold Rush Trail (called by one writer, "the 33 meanest miles in history") from Skagway Alaska to Lake Bennet, British Columbia. He continues to be active in the Changepoint Consulting group (changepoint.org)

www.ingramcontent.com/pod-product-compliance
Lightning Source LLC
Chambersburg PA
CBHW031202270326
41931CB00006B/368